T0098547

Flipping the Fairytale

FLIPPING *the* FAIRYTALE

The Six Magic Keys to Unlocking Your Relationship Potential

CINDI ZAREE

NEW YORK

LONDON • NASHVILLE • MELBOURNE • VANCOUVER

Flipping the Fairytale

Six Magic Keys to Unlocking Your Relationship Potential

© 2018 Cindi Laree

All rights reserved. No portion of this book may be reproduced, stored in a retrieval system, or transmitted in any form or by any means—electronic, mechanical, photocopy, recording, scanning, or other—except for brief quotations in critical reviews or articles, without the prior written permission of the publisher.

Published in New York, New York, by Morgan James Publishing in partnership with Difference Press. Morgan James is a trademark of Morgan James, LLC.
www.MorganJamesPublishing.com

The Morgan James Speakers Group can bring authors to your live event. For more information or to book an event visit The Morgan James Speakers Group at www.TheMorganJamesSpeakersGroup.com.

ISBN 9781683507468 paperback
ISBN 9781683507475 eBook
Library of Congress Control Number: 2017913507

Cover Design by:
Megan Whitney
megan@creativeninjadesigns.com

Interior Design by:
Chris Treccani
www.3dogcreative.net

In an effort to support local communities, raise awareness and funds, Morgan James Publishing donates a percentage of all book sales for the life of each book to Habitat for Humanity Peninsula and Greater Williamsburg.

Get involved today! Visit
www.MorganJamesBuilds.com

To Kaitlyn, Ashley, and Nicholas:

May you never give up on your dreams until you have created
your Happily Ever After.

Love,

Mommy

Table of Contents

Introduction		*ix*
Chapter 1	Lady-in-waiting, Waiting	1
Chapter 2	The Six Magic Keys to Unlocking Your Relationship Potential	15
Chapter 3	Are You Ready for the Ball?	21
Chapter 4	Mirror, Mirror on the Wall, Why in Relationships Do I Stumble and Fall?	31
Chapter 5	Where There Is Smoke, Beware of the Dragon	45
Chapter 6	Where Is the Knight in Shining Armor to Save this Damsel in Distress?	57
Chapter 7	Unlocking the Magic of Self- Love Through Failed Relationships	67
Chapter 8	Don't Be Fooled by the Frog Prince	77
Chapter 9	When You Run Out of Fairy Dust	85
Chapter 10	Becoming the Queen of Hearts	89
Afterword		*95*
Further Reading		*109*

Acknowledgments   *111*
About the Author   *115*
Thank You   117

Introduction

"Once Upon a Time." Every great fairytale started out with these words. Young girls read these words, watched Disney movies, and dreamed of someday marrying a Prince, becoming a Princess, and living Happily Ever After. As we grew into teenagers we watched romantic comedies and waited for our Prince to come and whisk us away from our ordinary life to something magical. We listened to power ballads and sang our hearts out waiting for our dream come true.

Then something strange happened as we got older: some of us met, fell in love, and began a significant relationship with who we thought was Prince Charming. In the beginning we felt like this was going to be something special, something mystical. That our lives would magically transform into something spectacular now that we had our Prince. Turns out he drank too much, spent too much time in his man cave, or thought that he knew everything about everything. We couldn't talk to him. He became more ogre than Prince – or maybe he was never a Prince at all, just a frog. Regardless, we did not become Princesses.

And so we find ourselves, later in life, still searching for the fairytale ending we had hoped for when we were younger. Only now we look and feel a little older, a little more haggard, or a little more tired than the fresh-faced Princesses we dreamed of becoming in our youth. The girl in the ball gown and glass slipper who could turn heads, or could at least swing an invitation to the ball. We are watching more Lifetime Movie Network and less Hallmark Channel because we have realized that our high school sweetheart isn't going to magically appear, divorced and irrevocably in love with us, at our 20-year class reunion. Nor is the former boy next door going to realize after all these years that it was us he loved and walk away from his supermodel fiancée to whisk us away to Happily Ever After. That kind of thing literally only happens in movies.

There are plenty of amazing men (Princes) in this world, yet before we are able to connect with an amazing one, there must be a rite of passage or a test of worthiness that we women must pass before we are introduced to the good ones. It is as if we must survive the encounters with the Village Idiots, Dragons, Knights in Shining Armor, and Frog Princes before we unlock the door to the land of Princes. These four groups are distinct archetypes of men that we meet while out on the dating market. Their defining characteristics will be discussed in depth later in the book.

It is difficult when navigating the archetypes. We can get lost in the relationship forest and forget what we were looking for, or, worse, begin to question if Prince Charming even exists anymore. We are frustrated looking for the real Princes and the magical connections. We consider giving up – at this point, we would be happy with a stable boy willing to respond with, "As you wish" as we cannot find a Prince. Where is the man who will make us a Princess? Where is the fairytale ending that we dreamed about in our youth?

It sucks to be a hopeless romantic. Not only are we faced with fears of being alone forever, but also the loneliness and frustration of that can carry over into so many other parts of our lives. Don't we deserve to be Princesses? Don't we deserve a dream-come-true relationship? It can be downright depressing to not have a Prince of our own, especially when we are surrounded by happy couples, and are one of the only singles in our group of friends or family. Sure, being a single lady is great for girls' night out, but when our coupled friends want to bring their husbands or significant others, we face the frustration of either not being included in the event, or the perpetual shame of "Just find a date and come with us!" If we could find dates that easily, we probably wouldn't be single. Don't get us started on our family events. How many times can we be patted on the hand by Aunt Betty as she says, "It's ok, honey, someday your Prince will come, maybe if you _____." (Insert horrible comment here: went to church, lost some weight, changed your hair, weren't so picky, etc. You name it, she has said it.)

The worst part is when our family reminds us of everyone else in the world that has come out of a break-up or divorce and easily found someone. "Did you know that Sally Smith's divorce was final two months ago? She's already engaged to the blacksmith over by the town square. You are just as smart and pretty as she is, and you have a nicer carriage. Maybe you should have gone out with him?" It makes family activities almost unbearable. It is hard to feel like we belong anywhere. Not with our friends, not with our families. Constantly feeling like the third wheel when we go out, or questioning why we can't find a Prince. Why is it that love happens for some women in an instant? But others, we must trudge through the enchanted woods hoping to stumble upon our Prince.

We feel bitter; the dream of Happily Ever After feels tarnished. At the same time, we become victims of self-deprecation and loathing: *why is this happening to me?* We are also developing a secret (and in some cases not-so-secret) obsession with dating and still trying to find our Prince. We daydream about how our lives would be different, how they would be easier if we had our Prince by our side. What it would finally be like to go to the ball. If our friends wanted to go on a couples date, boom! Guess who has someone to go with! Need someone to love you, hold you, and say you are beautiful? Need someone to talk to, cuddle with, and make love with? We have someone! There are so many basic needs that can be fulfilled by having a Prince by our side. For example, companionship, splitting the bills and responsibilities, having a confidante, etc. Then there is the romance and the passion side: someone to bring us flowers, remember our birthday, take us out for a romantic dinner on our anniversary, someone to say "I love you!" and "I like your butt." Having a Prince Charming and becoming his Princess is a fundamental need for the hopeless romantic. Life would truly be a dream with Him by our side living Happily Ever After, and right now our life is bordering on a lonely nightmare.

Sometimes we focus so much on our expectations and how we think things should be, as well as dwell on the mistakes we made in our past, that we forget to enjoy and appreciate the power we hold in creating our Happily Ever After. More specifically, we blame our lonely nightmare of a life on not having a Prince and not being a Princess, when the reality is, are we living the life we need to attract our Prince? Sometimes it isn't about finding a Prince to love us and make us a Princess. It's about becoming the person who is going to attract the Prince among the frogs and co-create our Happily Ever After.

Indulge in this fantasy for a moment:

Once upon a time, there was a Lady-in-waiting. She, like most of us, was not born into royalty. However she always dreamed that her Prince would come and make her a Princess. The Lady-in-waiting married a merchant man. During their marriage, she became consumed with keeping the cottage and all things family on track for their Happily Ever After. She dreamed that one day they would have a castle and the Happily Ever After that she had always dreamed of. Somewhere in the day-to-day of things, the Lady-in-waiting forgot what it was that she enjoyed, what brought passion and meaning into her life. The Lady-in-waiting forgot that she was to be a Princess, in fact, she began to feel as though she was turning into an ogre.

After failed attempts at rescuing her fairytale, the merchant and the Lady-in-waiting called it quits. A Royal Decree was signed for the dissolution of their marriage.

Now, as a single woman, the Lady-in-waiting set out to find her fairytale ending, one with passion and romance. She was committed to finding a Prince, because marrying a Prince is how you become a Princess. The Lady-in-waiting searched the kingdom in hopes of finding her Prince, but the Prince eluded her. The Lady-in-waiting sought out mystics and sages to help her find her Prince. Each bore a similar message: the Lady-in-waiting would not attract her Prince until she created a passion-filled life and transformed *herself* into a Princess.

The Lady-in-waiting, eager to transform, began to travel the kingdom in search of her passion. She visited the healing waters of Bath; she discovered divine gifts within herself. She began playing croquet, a game that she had enjoyed in her youth, but had never found time to play while she was with the merchant. She started to write poetry and sing songs at the tavern on karaoke night; she began to live a passion-filled life. It was strange, but as she earnestly sought the transformation to help her find her Prince, she realized one day that she no longer felt lonely. She no longer feared a Saturday night alone. She was at peace. The Lady-in-waiting was healing through the magic of this passion-filled life and self-care in hopes of transitioning to a Princess. In reward of her efforts, the Lady-in-waiting was waiting no more. She was able to create a new definition of Happily Ever After that included manifesting new talents, hobbies, relationships, and the fairytale ending she had always imagined as a young girl.

The Lady-in-waiting was just like each of us at the beginning of her journey. She embraced the *Six Magic Keys to Unlocking Your Relationship Potential* and transformed into a Princess to live her Happily Ever After.

Chapter 1

Lady-in-waiting, Waiting

I was the Lady-in-waiting looking to find my version of Happily Ever After. Not to mention I was a hopeless romantic. In my specific situation, not only did fairytales and Disney movies play into my unrealistic expectations about love, romance, and Happily Ever After, so did my family's faith – I was born and raised in the Mormon church, and this was a contributing factor to my fairytale psychosis. As a young woman growing up, I learned from the church that if you live worthy and marry a return missionary, you will have your Dream Come True life, a version that also included all time and eternity. I am sure that these teachings are not unique to the Mormons, as I have often heard my clients or friends wish that they would have married or are looking for a "good" Catholic, Christian, or Jewish man. It is a choice that religious leaders hope that we will all make; there can be benefits to a shared, faith-based marriage.

Living worthy meant making good choices, being a good example, living life in accordance to the religious teachings, etc. I tried to do that, but the practical application was difficult. I had boyfriends in high school, and kissed several others that weren't boyfriends. I certainly made my fair share of good and "iffy" decisions as I exercised my freedom of choice. Consequently I wasn't the best Mormon out there, but I definitely wasn't the worst. I knew the promise: make good choices + marry a return missionary = live Happily Ever After. That didn't happen for me.

I made some bad choices; I dated a Dragon. A Dragon, as we will talk about later in this book, is part of the Dragon Archetype. Men in this category are the masters of illusion and magic. They have a special gift for deception and manipulation.

My first Dragon appeared in my life was when I was 20 and a doe-eyed girl working my first job in retail. I had just moved to the Kingdom after a few years at community college. He was a near-perfect specimen! A Prince, I was almost certain. Whenever he was around, it was as if he had cast a spell on me and the mystical fog entranced me, or maybe it was hormones. Either way, he was muscular, handsome, well-moisturized, and he was interested in me. I had never met a Dragon like this, let alone ever been asked out on a date by one. When he asked me out, I probably should have known that he was too good to be true, but let's be honest. He was intriguing and smooth, so smooth. We actually went on a few dates and with each one I was more excited, and continued to buy into the fairytale more and more. He told me wonderful things. He talked of growing up Mormon, but deciding later that he didn't fit the Mormon ideals. I could sympathize with that. He talked of possibly returning to the church if he met the right girl. I could be that girl! He made me feel like I was the Princess of his world. With each date he lured me further and further into his lair. I think the naïve girl in me saw him as the Prince I never thought that I would have. He was smart, handsome, and eloquent. My head was so far in the clouds, I didn't even realize that his lair wasn't a castle, but a dungeon. To him I was just another virgin to sacrifice to his own indulgent needs.

Then it happened. I was date raped. I couldn't believe it. He wasn't a Prince; he was a Dragon, a dream-stealing, fairytale-crushing Dragon. My glass slipper shattered, and my dreams of a fairytale were crushed. He burned me that night; saving myself for my future husband was no longer an option. He took that from me, along with all of the dreams of what forever and Happily Ever After could look like. He did it so well, not only was I devastated, but I also felt like it was all my fault. I should have known better. I should have made better choices. At this point in my life I was a damsel in despair, so my thoughts were immediately self-deprecating. I told myself that he was too handsome for someone like me. He was too smooth, I should have seen through his lies. In retrospect I noticed the smoke in his lair, but didn't think the fire could burn me. This Dragon not only took my virginity against my will, but also took my self- respect, and he did it in a way that prevented me from talking about it or reporting it. I was ashamed. After all, I knew better. This is what happens when you don't stick to the plan, make good choices + date a return missionary = live Happily Ever After. This was my fault.

From that point on in my life, I knew that I wasn't worthy of the fairytale. This is possibly when the original obsession to find a Prince who would love me began. What was crazy is that I knew that for the majority of the population, pre-marital sex was not a big deal, especially when there was a traumatic event associated with it. It most definitely should have been forgiven. But in order to gain forgiveness, that would mean talking about it, and I just couldn't do that. I didn't want my friends or family to look at me disgusted or worse in pity, even though I was pretty sure that everyone could see my scarlet letter appearing on my skin. "U" for Unclean, "W" for Whore, "S" for Slut, or Stupid – no matter what the letter was, the feelings resonated all the time, and I wasn't going to talk about it.. After losing everything to the Dragon's fire, I had to revamp my fairytale. The guys I dated in college were currently serving missions; they were not going to want me. They would want a pristine Lady-in-waiting, one that had the strength and sense to make good decisions and stay out of harm's way. I left that enchanted forest and had to find a new dream come true.

I spent a good portion of the next year feeling like I had blown my chance at the fairytale. That I would never have my dream come true romance because I made mistakes. Then, in a serendipitous moment, I met a merchant and fell madly in love – let's be honest, I am a hopeless romantic, how else would I fall in love? The merchant thought that I was something special too, and 11 months later, we were married, 24 hours before the birth of our beautiful baby girl. Unfortunately, there was no magic of conception and spontaneous birth, I got pregnant two months into our dating. Sure, it wasn't a conventional "dream come true" start, but it was something. Once I held my baby girl it was hard for me to feel like this was anything but the right path for me. I was ready and waiting for my Happily Ever After. The marriage had its peaks and valleys, and I kept waiting, but after the birth of our son, it was obvious to this Lady-in-waiting that our marriage would never amount to the Happily Ever After I desperately wanted.

My divorce from the merchant boiled down to irreconcilable differences. I was tired of dreaming and wishing for the romantic fairytale that the merchant thought was unrealistic and ridiculous. I wanted a marriage where I felt special. I wanted to feel loved, appreciated, and honored as the Princess in my home. Instead, I felt oppressed, like I was more nanny, housemaid, and cook than co-ruler of the kingdom. Then there were other basic issues that plague married life, such as finances, time, intimacy, etc. During the separation we both said and did some things we weren't proud of, like indulging in screaming matches, hurtful emails, name calling, etc.

After our divorce, I wanted to show the merchant that I was capable and worthy of having the type of relationship I desired, a relationship that he could not or would not give me. I wanted to feel special. I wanted to be treated like a Princess.

My expectations of Happily Ever After were, I thought, realistic. I wanted romance. I had wanted to get flowers for special occasions, or even for no occasion at all. Instead, I had a price tag hanging on a rearview mirror as proof that at one time in our marriage the merchant had bought me flowers. I had expectations of intimacy. I had wanted someone to snuggle me and hold me throughout the night as I slept. Instead I got someone who wanted his own room because my breathing disturbed him. Don't get me wrong, I know that there were things that he desired also, that I wasn't willing at the time to do.

Was finding a romantic, loving relationship so difficult? Sure, it didn't work with the merchant, but I wasn't willing to give up on my dream come true. I wanted the Prince and the fairytale marriage. I began to seek out my Happily Ever After. Forget the Mormon formula, I was disenchanted with "marry a return missionary and live Happily Ever After." I had missed that chance, plus I had witnessed firsthand that not all faith-based marriages work out the way they are planned.

So my focus shifted to finding a good man. And when I say "finding," I should probably say that I was obsessed with having a new relationship. Not the good kind of obsessed where you are goal-focused, I was like a Lifetime Movie Network character, totally crazy and trying to find somebody to love me. Now that I was single, I thought it would be easy to move forward and find a Prince. It wasn't. It was work. It was tears, it was kissing Frogs, fighting or being fooled by a Dragon, and having my heart broken more than once by a Knight in Shining Armor. In fact, it took me close to five years trying to wrangle a Prince to unlock my relationship potential and become not just the Princess, but eventually the Queen. Although it may have been necessary for me to struggle, if there is a chance that you can relate to my story, my shame, my mistakes, and the lessons I learned, perhaps I can save you from feeling like a crazy woman and help you move faster into that Happily Ever After relationship you desire.

After my divorce was final, I opened an account on Match.com. Where "1 in 12 matches end in a relationship." What they don't tell you in the ad is that 9 of 12 end with a stalker, freak show, or unsolicited pictures of a man's junk. But if you can wade through the liars and the cheats and hang in long enough, you may find something. Since I was obsessed with finding love, I stayed in there. Some of my first connections dating online were Village Idiots. These men tended to be beggars or boys looking for brothels, versus actual relationship material. Sure, they didn't put that stuff on their profile, otherwise I wouldn't have talked to them (I think), but still it didn't take long to know that their intentions were significantly different than mine.

I remember specifically "Pappa Bear 69" (I know the name alone should have been a sign, but I was obsessed. I was focused on finding a man, any man, not on finding the right man). PappaBear69 was very interested in me immediately. I should have known he was a Village Idiot. He wanted to meet in person, and to be quite honest, I thought that was refreshing. Texting and emailing back and forth really didn't give me any idea "who" a person actually was. I agreed to meet him at a mall near my house. I had read about the dangers, and many of my friends had warned me about online dating safety. I had been very careful not to give my last name, address, or too much information about my children or my family in the event that things didn't go well. On the morning of our meeting, PappaBear69 texted me: "My homie needs to use my car today, I told him he can just drop me off at your house, Aight? Oh yeah, do you cook?"

Wait! What? No it wasn't ok, I didn't know anything about this guy, I certainly wasn't prepared to have him in my home, and seriously, do I cook? Of all the things that he could ask, he wants to know if I will cook for him? Drop him off at my house? Not yet, maybe not ever! I responded, "No that doesn't work for me." He instantly freaked out and started accusing me of having other guys on the side. Telling me that the only reason I wouldn't want him to come over for the day was because I was hiding something. He proceeded to call me a player and a liar, and to call into integrity everything I had shared with him. Then he began to apologize and beg to be allowed to come over, he was sorry. He was just used to being burned by other women, but he realized he didn't know me well enough to jump to conclusions. That is why we needed to get together that day. He was trying to manipulate me into letting him come over. No thank you! We didn't end up going out that day. For some, that would have been the end of PappaBear69, but not me.

Although we didn't meet that day, I still wasn't counting him out as an option.

I was so caught up in finding someone, I was ignoring huge red flags. If it weren't for my Fairy Godmother (aka my little sister) and her intervention to save me during those first dating experiences, this story could have had an entirely different outcome. Her greatest save was probably with the next guy, Jack. I was trying to avoid issues similar to PappaBear69, so I was texting much more, having more in-depth conversations about likes/dislikes, and talking about my children (although being very guarded in the information provided). Jack and I had been talking for almost a month, and we decided to go on a date and meet in person. I really thought that I was falling for him. He seemed to be so sweet, and so sincere. Going on a date was merely a formality, not just for me, but for him also. He told me that he was going to be signing a new lease at an apartment but would only sign for 6 months, because he wanted to be able to move things forward with us at that time. We hadn't actually met in person at this point, and sure, it seemed too soon. But how romantic was that! I liked him, he liked me, and he was already planning our Happily Ever After together. I was one lucky girl.

Maybe not so lucky. A week before our date, I broke my elbow in an unfortunate accident. When I told him I had to cancel our date, he went from Prince Charming to the Big Bad Wolf. He huffed and he puffed, and he called me horrible names and told me I was like every other woman out there. Just playing games with his heart. I honestly couldn't believe what I was reading. I apologized and told him that I was serious. I even offered to send him a picture of the x-ray. I wanted to go out with him, but at the time, I couldn't even button my own pants if I had to use the restroom. I wanted nothing more than to impress him on our date, and with the pain and awkwardness of the cast, I didn't think that I was ready to go on a date. He was still angry. It didn't seem to matter. The harder I tried to explain, the worse the insults became. I hadn't intended on rejecting him. I just needed another week or two to heal and get out of the splint. I was shocked. I called my Fairy Godmother immediately, and she said, "Good riddance." She told me he was trouble and to stay away from him. I was hurt, possibly even devastated at the time. Between the breakup and the broken elbow, I felt I was at an all-time low. It had been six months since my divorce. I hadn't found my Prince, and the Merchant was living his new Happily Ever After with a new Lady-in-waiting. Ugh!

About two weeks after Jack freaked out on me, he texted me to apologize. As it turns out there were some mitigating issues with his ex that had caused him to lash out so harshly at me. I told him he had hurt me, and that I didn't know if I could trust him with my heart again. He promised that we would take things very slowly and that he would earn back my trust. He wanted very much to be with me, and create a good life together.

Against the advice of my Fairy Godmother, I told Jack I would give him a second chance. He was ecstatic. We were back on again! Immediately he asked if we could go ahead and meet in person as our relationship up to this point was only text messaging. My elbow was mostly better, I was only in a sling now, and could successfully button and unbutton my pants if needed. So I agreed to meet him over the weekend.

On the Tuesday before we were to meet, he asked if I could meet him for coffee. He'd had a bad day. I told him that unfortunately I had plans with my friend Tim. Tim was a Knight in Shining Armor who had shown up in my life exactly when I needed a miracle. He was a trusted friend, and a loyal Knight. Jack freaked out again. He told me that Tim was a wolf in sheep's clothing, and that Jack was my sheep dog, and it was his job to keep me safe from the wolves. I am sorry! Where did that come from? Trust me, if anyone needed protection in the friendship between me and Tim, it was Tim. I often let my feelings for him go too far into fairytale land, and I would end up broken-hearted. But never in the years I had known him had he ever done anything that would lead me to believe he was anything other than a loyal supportive friend.

The more I tried to explain this, the crazier Jack became. He told me I was naïve, and that I had poor judgment in men. That I needed to trust that he knew what was best for me. The warnings from my Fairy Godmother came flooding over me: the guy sounds crazy, don't talk to him again, you deserve better, you aren't a child, you deserve to be treated with respect, etc. It was definitely time to be rid of Jack for good. I told him I was done, that he had blown his chance, and then I quit texting him. If I quit texting him, I thought, he will go away. He will get the hint that I am not interested, right?

Wrong! So wrong! Over the course of two hours, I received 42 text messages and 15 phone calls from Jack. He wanted to talk to me. He needed to explain. I didn't respond. I needed back-up. I called my Fairy Godmother, and told her what had happened. After some gentle shaming, she told me to figure out exactly what information he knew about me. As the hours passed, the text messages became angrier and angrier. We also did some research online about Jack just to see what we were dealing with.

No kidding, we found him on mugshots.com! He had multiple restraining orders against him from different women and pending charges for assault and assault with intent to injure. I wasn't even sure what that was, but I knew it couldn't be good for me. The text messages and calls kept coming, and I realized that I had an angry, Grade A stalker on my hands. Fortunately, after reviewing all of our messages, I realized that he didn't have any specifics on me as to where I lived or where my kids went to school. He did know where I worked, and unfortunately a Google search could easily reveal my name and work address. I was panicked. The threats kept coming in via text, the calls were adding up. What had I gotten myself into? Had I wanted a relationship so badly that I had no regard for my safety or doing my research? Jack was undeniably the Big Bad Wolf.

Fortunately my Fairy Godmother devised a rescue plan, and called Jack from her phone. She left a message stating that he needed to quit calling her daughter "Jessica," that Jessica was grounded from her phone until further notice, and by the way, he didn't sound 17. My phone blew up with phone calls from Jack. They went unanswered. He finally called my Fairy Godmother. He began to explain that he had been having a relationship with the owner of the phone, Cindi. That she was 35 and had three kids and worked for a school. My sister responded that the phone had belonged to her daughter Jessica for five years now, and that she knew Cindi, but wasn't sure what he was talking about. She asked him to cease and desist contact with Jessica, as she was a minor, and clearly he was not. She respectfully asked him to stop or she would involve the authorities. Brilliant! The last thing a man with pending criminal charges against him wanted was to give the police another opportunity to talk to him. He said he didn't understand. He was certain that Jessica/Cindi was an adult that he was in a relationship with. My sister told him she would get to the bottom of this and call him back. After about 20 minutes she called him and explained that Jessica and her friend (Cindi's daughter) had watched a movie on Disney channel where two girls use a fake dating profile to attract a boyfriend for their mother. The girls meant no harm, and apologized for what had happened. She assured him that the girls would be punished accordingly. But at this point he must cease and desist contact. Jack argued that he knew that Cindi was real. That it was impossible that it could all be a scam. My Fairy Godmother assured him that I was real, that I had no knowledge of the situation, and that she would be letting me know as soon as she hung up the phone. Jack was angry, but given his history, that appeared to be his go-to emotion. I dodged a bullet that day. I never heard from Jack again. In fact, I closed my online dating account that day. If I was going to find my Happily Ever After, it was going to be somewhere else. There had to be a better way.

Chapter 2

The Six Magic Keys to Unlocking Your Relationship Potential

I was in a situation where I knew I had to make changes, I was willing to make changes, and yet as I moved forward to make changes, I kept getting lost or caught up in the drama that was my life at the time. I had been a hopeless romantic for 30+ years. Changing that overnight was not going to be easy. At times I felt like I was wandering through the forest like Moses in the desert, looking for scraps of manna and an ounce of water to quench my relationship thirst. Sometimes a step forward would turn into an avalanche backslide, and I would get discouraged.

I spent a lot of time in self-evaluation mode. Asking myself if I deserved a fairytale relationship, why I kept attracting the same type of men, none of them Princes, and what it would take for me to get my dream come true. My obsession to have a relationship had been turned down a notch or two, it was now more burning desire than obsession. After all, Jack had made me literally afraid for my life. I don't know what would have happened if my sister's cover story had blown up. I needed to get right with myself and the Universe and figure out what I was doing wrong.

I started doing market research (yes, that would be more online dating), journaling, and making small changes in my life that would later help me discover the keys to unlocking my relationship potential. I was looking for guys, any guys, and I thought that like a fisherman, if I were to cast the biggest net possible, I would be able to catch several men. Surely one of them would be my Prince.

Admittedly, I floundered in the beginning of my search. I would have some small victories, but more often defeats. It was a learning process taught through the school of hard knocks. There were a few Knights in Shining Armor, a Fairy Godmother or two, lots of hope and trust, and fairy dust that helped to ease the pain of defeat. But in the end I found it. The answers to my dating woes could be found in the archetypes of men I was attracting. I realized what it was in me (obsessive behavior, low self-esteem, and over-focus on quantity vs. quality) that was calling in the Village Idiots, Dragons, Knights in Shining Armor, and the Frog Princes. As each of these archetypes presented himself, though, I was given another key to unlock my relationship potential. I realized each of these keys unlocked the secrets to passionate love that I had never known as a Lady-in-waiting.

Keys in hand, I was able to heal my hopeless romantic, become a Princess, and find a passion-filled life. You guessed it, ladies, I rewrote the formula for love and created my Happily Ever After. I have even created a diagnostic quiz to help women identify the archetypes they attract to expedite the transformation process. Now I know that it is my sacred duty, my sworn oath, to share the magic keys of love with other Ladies-in-waiting and hopeless romantics out there who, like me, were struggling to find their dream-come-true relationship. Join me on the enchanted journey, as we collect the keys and unlock the secrets to maximizing your relationship potential.

The Six Magic Keys to Unlocking Your Relationship Potential

1. Are You Ready for the Ball?

2. Mirror Mirror on the Wall, Why in Relationships Do I Stumble and Fall?

3. Where There Is Smoke, Beware of the Dragons

4. Where Is the Knight in Shining Armor to Save this Damsel in Distress?

5. Unlocking the Magic of Self-Love Through Failed Relationships

6. Don't Be Fooled by the Frog Prince

1. **Are You Ready for the Ball?** Everyone wants to live Happily Ever After, so it is difficult when our fairytale isn't working out. It is even more difficult if we aren't honest with ourselves about what we want, and what we are willing to work for. If we are truly passionate about having our dream-come-true relationship, we have to be willing to make changes in our lives. We must put in the work. There must be some direction: goals, accountability, follow-through, and forgiveness. Otherwise we risk being forever lost in the thorn bushes of bad relationships, our dreams unrealized. Getting ready for the ball is about making a choice and doing the work. It is about showing up in our life, and making things happen. We must do this ourselves; no one is going to hand us our dreams in a heart-shaped box. Even Cinderella had to scrub the floors and put up with her stepsisters' abusive idiocy before she was ready for the ball.

2. **Mirror Mirror on the Wall, Why in Relationships Do I Stumble and Fall?**

By identifying and discovering the traits of the Village Idiot Archetype, I was able to find the key to unlock the magic of the Law of Attraction. It all starts with belief. The Law of Attraction tells us that where our thoughts go, this is what we will manifest. Why is this important? Well, ladies, if we want to attract Prince Charming in our life, we must put some serious thought into the kind of Prince we want and why. It's important that we shift our mindset from what we *don't* want to what we *do* want. It is so easy for us to get so caught up in negativity, frustration, and dwelling on the things that we don't have that we lose focus on the things that we desire or want to have in our lives. This mental shift away from negativity and frustration to more positively guided thoughts like, "What would I rather have instead?" is an essential key to success in creating your Happily Ever After.

3. **Where There Is Smoke, Beware of the Dragon.** Discovering the Dragon Archetype, and unfortunately being burned, helped me find the important key to Manifesting/ Setting Boundaries. As we shift our mindset away from the negativity and frustration, it's important that we create positive guided thoughts with a projected ideal outcome. This is basically the concept of manifestation. Manifesting is a fancy way of saying we set goals and create a plan for achieving them. Setting Boundaries is where we give ourselves the space that we need to make the necessary changes to achieve our goals. Manifesting and setting boundaries are the check and balance essentials to creating your dream come true.

4. **Where Is the Knight in Shining Armor to Save this Damsel in Distress?** In order for us to move forward, it's important that we are actively manifesting the positive things in our lives. This encompasses setting goals and envisioning our success in accomplishing them. But we must be careful of setting expectations of "how" something will be accomplished. Sometimes when we want something so badly, we become overly focused on how it will happen, and it is those expectations and

attempts to control the outcome that are limiting our ability to achieve those goals. Releasing expectations allows the magic to happen. Yes, we need to take action on our goals and even set healthy boundaries for ourselves and others, but we also need to allow faith, trust, and a dash of pixie dust to guide us to our fairytale ending.

5. **Unlocking the Magic of Self-Love Through Failed Relationships.** Sometimes on the road to Happily Ever After we find that something we thought was our Dream Come True was instead a temporary solution, a stop-gap on the way to living a true passion-filled life. We recognize that being happy or finding happiness isn't something we do externally. Happiness, joy, passion, and romance all radiate different forms of self-love. When we have this self-love, our lives are infused with passion and romance. We transform ourselves in order to attract a Happily Ever After in all aspects of our life.

6. **Don't Be Fooled by the Frog Prince.** Even in our best attempts at being successful, we are still learning a new process and a different way of thinking and being that will take practice. It can often seem overwhelming when we look at where we are vs. where we want to be. It is essential that instead of being discouraged, we make small changes and adjustments to keep us on track for achieving our goals. Noticing the red flags, taking appropriate actions, and trusting our own discernment will help protect the castle walls from invasion while we are in the creation process.

Chapter 3

Are You Ready
for the Ball?

It is easy to become overwhelmed in the search for love and Happily Ever After. It is even easier to list all of the possible reasons why we haven't found our Prince Charming.

Reasons Why There Is No Prince

1. Princes aren't real!

2. Boys are dumb.

3. All the nice guys are already taken.

4. I am too _____ (fat, thin, ugly, intimidating, shy, outgoing, opinionated).

5. Men only want to hook up, not date.

6.   Men are pigs.

7.   I blew my chance at real love.

8.   I don't deserve happiness.

Finding the negatives in a situation is often easier than focusing on the opportunities for us to grow or change. This requires us to take an honest look at ourselves and admit that maybe, just maybe, we haven't found what we are looking for either because we don't know what that is, or we are so caught up wallowing in our self-pity or self-loathing that we haven't done the work to get it. We are missing three key elements for success: Accountability, Forgiveness, and Doing the Work.

Accountability

Accountability is about shifting the mindset from being a victim of circumstances to acknowledging that we are powerful creators and manifestors of the magic in our lives. Accountability is about taking responsibility for the energy we brought to the relationship and discerning whether we are, actively or passively, working on our goals. Accountability is about making choices in our lives and actively contributing to the outcome.

Forgiveness

We are all operating under different beliefs and different stress levels. As we become more accountable for our choices, often we are reminded of the poor choices we made previously in our lives. In order to move forward and create a Happily

Ever After, we have to forgive ourselves – and others – for our previous actions or choices made when we were operating under different beliefs.

> "Do the best you can until you know better.
> Then when you know better, do better."
> **MAYA ANGELOU**

Forgiveness is about freeing ourselves so that we are open to receiving the blessings and benefits that come from creating through power manifesting and law of attraction.

Do the Work

Doing the work allows us to become the type of people we want to date. Are we ready for the ball? The interesting thing about fairytales that sort of slips buy us when we are caught up in the anticipation of the Prince and the Happily Ever After is this: Prior to their dreams coming true, those ladies had to go through some pretty tough times. Cinderella lost her parents and became the maid for her wicked stepmother and stepsisters. Snow White had a hit put out on her by an evil Queen. Her only refuge was to spend her days in servitude to seven sweaty little men. Even then, she was almost poisoned. Rapunzel was kidnapped, locked in a tower, and forced to live alone until she was rescued. Sleeping Beauty was cursed and then consequently forced to live with strangers because her parents didn't invite everyone to her baby shower. The point in all of this is that in order for us to reap the benefits of the Prince, the castle, and the Happily Ever After, we must do the work. We must ask ourselves, "Am I ready for the ball?" If our Fairy Godmother were to show up right now with the shoes, the dress, and the carriage, would we be ready for the ball? Or would we stay back because even with all of those things, we aren't ready for Prince Charming? At the beginning of the chapter we listed reasons why we haven't found a Prince. Some were about the Prince, but some of those were specific to our preparedness for the ball. "I am too _____." When we begin to do the self-work and forgive, we realize that the excuse "I am too_____" has everything to do with how we feel about ourselves, and nothing to do with finding a Prince.

Cinderella was ready for the ball. She did the work; she made a dress with help from her furry friends. She didn't self-destruct when her stepmother rejected her. She was a beautiful person inside and out. She was prepared to go to the ball without divine intervention. After she had done everything that she could possibly do to prepare for the ball – the chores, the prep work for her stepmother and stepsisters, etc. – that is when the magic happened. In order for the magic to happen in our lives, we must do the work. We must be willing to make changes and put in the time and effort to become the girl worthy of a Prince.

> "If you really want to do something, no one can stop you.
> But if you really don't want to do something,
> no one can help you."
> - **JAMES A. OWEN,** *DRAWING OUT DRAGONS*

Tina's Story

I remember working one night with Tina. She was frustrated by not making faster progress. She had taken all the steps to create the new her. She had divorced her deadbeat husband, gotten a stable job making good money, and joined a few singles groups. She was trying to date, but couldn't find someone who wasn't a psycho. Why hadn't her fairytale taken off?

Tina listed all the steps that she had taken over the 18 months since the divorce. When I asked her, "What have you done today to reach your goals? What are your goals? Have you written them down or are they in your head? Give me the specifics of what you are doing to be successful?" she told me she had no specific plan. She just wanted to meet a nice guy and live the dream. We talked about the importance of being accountable daily for accomplishing her goals. As we talked, she realized that she wasn't doing the work. She had hit a plateau. Tina and I agreed it was like she had gone to the fabric store and bought a lot of material and supplies, but just left it on the counter and waited for someone else to make her dress. In real life, there are not furry friends to come to your rescue. She had to do the work for herself, as do we all. If we aren't willing to do the work, then it's essential that we get real and get honest about where we are in our lives.

> "You are exactly where you want to be,
> otherwise you would change it."
> **- TIM GRANT**, *KNIGHT IN SHINING ARMOR.*

Are you ready for the ball? Honesty is essential to progress.

Do I know who I am and what I want in a relationship?

Many of us we are either exiting a long-term relationship, have never felt like we had a successful relationship to begin with, or, as in my case, are so obsessed with proving we can have a relationship that we'll settle for a man, any man. When this is the case, it is often difficult to know who we are or what we truly desire in a relationship. Do the work, try practice dating, or just going out with groups of people, singles events, etc. Meet people and participate in activities, not specifically for finding your Prince Charming, but to gain experience. Often times, we get so caught up in finding a man we forget to be objective about whether this is the right kind of man for us.

Am I at a place of peace in my life?

When we're not, it's often difficult to admit. But when we are actively seeking companionship, we must look at where we are and determine whether we are in a place in our lives where we can dedicate the necessary time and effort it takes to have a loving, successful romantic relationship. Take into consideration the following: am I drama-free from my last relationship? Do I have any overwhelming tasks or projects I am currently committed to, like starting a new business, taking on lots of travel for work, going to school, or family commitments? Am I ready for the ball?

This isn't to say that until our children are raised, or we are successful in our careers we shouldn't be allowed to be in a relationship, but to take an honest look at the time and effort required to sustain our life, and if there is enough time and energy to devote to a new relationship.

There is nothing wrong with prioritizing our life to a place of peace, before we begin a new relationship.

This was difficult for me, as I wanted to have it all! I knew that I wasn't being fulfilled at my current job anymore, and I had a very strong pull to begin my own coaching business. I had worked with clients here and there, and was dedicated to helping them heal and reach their infinite potential. I was continuing to work on my own healing path, and was juggling a new relationship with a carpenter named John.

I knew the relationship had flaws. Among many, he wasn't honest with me. He had lied on his profile about his age. By the time I knew the truth, I had convinced myself that it was ok, because we appeared to be compatible on so many other levels. We would talk on the phone for hours at a time. In fact, that was our only option, because he lived out of state. I had gone to spend a weekend with him, and it was a lot of fun. Again, not perfect – it was clear we had very different mindsets on raising children and we grew up in different generations. But hey, he was interested in me, and I really liked the idea of being in a relationship.

About a week after my trip to visit him, I was attending a Ladies Healing Day where I met with a beautiful Native American Shaman woman who was helping me to clear my energy, and provide any messages from Spirit to help me on my journey. She talked to me about being conflicted and pulled in multiple directions. She told me that I could not have both a relationship and a new business. That it was my time to move forward with my business, and the doors of opportunity and development were opening to me. But I needed to decide. Relationships, much like children, need nurturing.

Ugh! That sucked. I was willing to make a go of a relationship, but I wanted to open my new business and be successful more than I wanted the relationship. It wasn't fair to him, either. So I made a choice to break it off. As it turned out, it was the best thing ever; he originally was going to move to Arizona within a few months. Then that never happened. Truth be known, that may have been a lie also, he had proven time and time again that he wasn't honest. So it was definitely in my highest and best interest to let it go.

Have I forgiven myself and others?

For some of us, this can be the most difficult question to answer. Forgiving ourselves is another way to make sure that we have stepped off of the emotional roller coaster and have made peace with who and where we are in life. We can't start a successful relationship if we are still beating ourselves up over things that happened previously in our lives or relationships.

Bringing that energy forward will most assuredly guarantee failure in a new relationship.

Create a healthy body mind and soul connection; find an accountability partner, hire a life coach to help facilitate progress; work with change modalities to guarantee success; look for spiritual guidance; meditate; invest in a journal and actively track your progress.

Chapter 4

Mirror, Mirror on the Wall, Why in Relationships Do I Stumble and Fall?

I asked the above question many times back when I was looking for answers to my relationship vertigo. To which the Magic Mirror responded, "Quit dating the Village Idiots, just a suggestion."

In the beginning of my once upon a time, I was obsessed with finding a new relationship. I did all the things that I thought I should do to get ready for the ball. I started on dating sites, I joined Meetup groups for my interests – anything that I thought would put me in a place to meet Prince Charming. I was already looking for a new relationship before I had time to land on my feet from my divorce. I guess you could say I was going to tuck and roll out of it, and keep moving.

The only problem with the tuck-and-roll philosophy is that sometimes when you tuck and roll, you may have sustained injuries from the last relationship that need to be assessed at the very least, if not land you in the hospital for some observation and healing time to make sure everything is in working order. In hindsight, I probably could have significantly reduced the time it took me to create my fairytale ending had I hit pause and not tried so hard to find another true love. But not me! I was invincible! Tuck and Roll, Baby! I hadn't really thought through my plan. I thought it was simple: find a Prince and live Happily Ever After. There was no real thought put into the type of Prince I wanted, I was simply determined to just get a man and work out the rest later.

My ability to think clearly and discern right from wrong was quite possibly still bouncing around in my head from the tuck-and-roll move, and I was acting out of pure adrenaline and with a singular focus: finding Prince Charming. I wasn't dishonest in my initial dating profile. I was vague. My pictures were current, my demographic information was correct. But when I answered the profile questions about my likes and dislikes, I was vague, I just went with generic answers, I wasn't looking for the right guy, I was trying to cast a wide net to capture any guy. I wasn't ready for the ball.

Now in my defense, anyone who has ever filled out a dating profile, whether it is 10 questions or 30, knows that it is difficult to accurately portray who you are with pre-canned questions. Do you like sports? Yes I do. But that doesn't necessarily mean that I am willing to devote my weekends to the couch or sports bar to cheer on overpaid athletes while they play with their respective balls.

Truth be told, I was not even in a place to be selective about what I did or didn't want in a relationship. I had been with my ex for 13 years, during which time the dating scene and its technology had changed exponentially since that last time I had been single. So in order to maximize my opportunities to find love, I went searching the Internet village. I found John and PappaBear69, along with several others, and I started to realize that they fit into the first archetype of men: the Village Idiots. Village Idiots are what can be considered low-hanging fruit. They are the guys who are most readily available when you begin your quest for romance. Much like I did initially, they are casting a wide net in the dating pond and hoping to catch something. Within the Village Idiots Archetype there are three subcategories: the Beggars, the boys looking for Brothels, and the Peasants.

Beggars

The Beggars can be a flattering and receptive group. They seem very interested in you and what you have to offer. In the end, I found them to be mostly needy, high-maintenance, or total push-overs. There's a reason why they are not picky.

I met one of them, Kevin, for breakfast one day. He was very nice and polite in our interactions. His profile was a 97% match with mine. I definitely was excited to meet him and see if he was my one in 12! We met at a café, and as we sat and talked, Kevin began to tell me about his recent divorce. His wife had cheated on him, and he was struggling to move on, but I seemed like exactly the girl that could help him through it. I was equal parts flattered and creeped out. We had just met, and up until this point in breakfast I had said maybe only 20 words. As the conversation evolved, he told me of the utter devastation he suffered by his wife, that he had even asked her to go to counseling, and offered to forgive her for her affair – no questions asked – if she would just come back to him. She would not take him back. He then proceeded to share with me his current salary and living expenses, along with the promise that any residual income in his check would be up for grabs to buy me nice things, take me on dates, or maybe a family vacation. He then went on to share that he was an excellent father, and that he would be happy to coach my children's teams, attend parent-teacher conferences, and love my kids like they were his own.

At this point, I was really creeped out. I tried to explain to Kevin that my kids would not enter into my dating equation for months, as I didn't want them to meet anyone until it was a serious relationship with real potential. I may have been obsessed with moving on, but my children still needed some time to adjust and heal. Kevin said he wasn't worried, that we had all the time in the world to evolve. He was just happy to have someone in his life now: a partner, a confidant, someone who would be there with him at his best and at his worst. I wasn't exactly sure if he was at his best or worst at that very moment. Kevin wanted a lot of the same things that I wanted in a relationship at the time, but when he said it, it sounded so desperate and needy. It was a huge turn-off for me. I needed to escape that date and never look back, and I did.

Boys Looking for Brothels

I found more than my share of boys looking for Brothels also, not just PappaBear69. It was honestly frightening the number of times I would read a profile for someone looking for "a special lady to spend the rest of my life with," and then, during the course of our conversation or even very quickly in the conversation, the questions would shift to how playful or adventurous I was in bed, requests to send nude pictures of myself, or, my personal favorite, sharing unsolicited pictures of their junk. Nothing says "Let's start a relationship!" quite like an up close and personal review of your goodies, right? These aren't guys who want to be in a relationship. They want to be in a brothel, randomly whoring about. Here Ye! Here Ye! Ladies, this is an important lesson to learn: Women tend to dabble with sex in hopes of having a relationship. Men will dabble with a relationship in hopes of having sex.

What exactly does that mean? He may be only pretending to want to date you, so that he can score! But ladies, we aren't off the hook that easily, we often make choices or justify some of our actions based on the idea that maybe if he samples the milk, he will want to "buy the cow." It is a story that we tell ourselves to make us feel better about our poor choices in men. Don't be afraid to leave them in the brothels. If that is ultimately where they want to take you, let them go at it alone.

Peasants

Peasants are guys we know are not what we dreamt about, but we are willing to settle for, because, well, we don't know where to find the good ones. Or maybe we don't even know if they exist anymore. Shortly after joining Match.com, I met Aaron. Aaron was a Peasant for me, but he could have likely been someone else's Prince Charming. When I was honest with myself, we just weren't compatible on several levels. Aaron was a less impressive version of my ex, and I almost missed all of the signs if it hadn't been for my Fairy Godmother/sister stepping in again to point out the blaring similarities between the two. What can I say, I was focused so much on getting to the ball that I didn't notice the invitation wasn't from my Prince.

The hard but simple truth is that if we find ourselves surrounded by Village Idiots, it's time to take a look in the mirror. This is basic Law of Attraction at work. Simply put, like attracts like. The energy that we put into a situation is exactly the energy we will receive or draw from the situation. Oh, nuts! You guessed it, ladies; I was surrounded by idiots, because I was putting out the idiot vibe. Obviously it was not my intention to attract these guys. But it was exactly the message I was sending by not having any guidance or criteria other than "Find Prince, Live Happily Ever After." In my dreams of hosting a tournament of Champions for my heart to find my Prince Charming, I forgot to require nobility. Consequently I allowed the Village Idiots to be contenders, and so the real Princes didn't even bother. A definite shift needed to happen and quickly if I was going to have my Happily Ever After. The key bestowed upon me from the Village Idiots Archetype was the power of the Law of Attraction.

Law of Attraction

Some people think the Law of Attraction is as simple as being a chalice-half-full kind of girl. But the Law of Attraction requires taking an honest look at all the elements of our lives and making sure that we are putting out the right vibe. Are we ready for the ball? Are we Prince Charming material? Or are we pretending to be a Princess when we are putting in serving wench effort? By that I mean: are we focused on improving ourselves and our situation? Are we scrambling but not making any progress? Or, like Tina, have we hit a plateau in life and are hoping for the best? I thought I was ready to be a Princess, but when I took an honest look in the mirror, I saw that I was scrambling, not improving.

It turned out that I was either chaotic or lazy or both – a perfect formula for attracting crazy. I had somehow found comfort in my misery. Not to mention the amount of attention that being miserable and dating the village idiots brought into my life. I had fantastic friends who would listen to me complain about my love life and tell me it would get better, to keep trying. They told me how they thought I was brave for putting myself out there, how they didn't know if they could even consider dating again, based on how horrible my experiences were.

I wore my misery like a badge of honor. Although I didn't necessarily want to have another bad date, I was confident that if I did, I could turn it into a small victory. We would commiserate, and celebrate the failures. My friends would encourage me to keep moving forward, tell me that I learned a good lesson, and affirm that I was strong, and that I would find my Prince eventually. I liked to hear their praise and affirmations even though in my heart of hearts, I knew I wasn't really doing anything differently. I definitely didn't value myself enough to step off of the crazy battlefield and allow myself to heal. I was a tuck-and-roll girl, and that was admirable! Or was it?

Before my divorce, when I was complaining about my marriage, Tim, the Knight in Shining Armor, would tell me, "You are living exactly the life you want to, otherwise you would change it." I could have given him a list of reasons why my marriage wasn't working out, none of which I felt at the time were my fault. But he was right, and the principle held true through my early dating period. Instead of continuing to commiserate with my friends, instead of being the tuck-and-roll girl, I needed to work on myself and become the Princess that deserves a Prince Charming.

I needed to take responsibility for my thoughts and my actions. I needed to make a choice: be honest with myself about what I wanted in my life and set goals, or continue wandering in the woods and hoping I would find my Prince. I also needed to practice the Law of Attraction in all areas of my life. I was going to have to release my addiction to drama and being the center of attention with my misery, and take steps forward in changing my thoughts. I needed to recognize that I wasn't a character in my fairytale. I was the author, and I had control over my story line.

I began being more selective about the guys that I dated or talked to. I tried meeting guys in different environments other than online dating forums. I revised my dating profile. I also began making mental lists of qualities or characteristics of my Prince Charming. If the Village Idiots had taught me anything, it was that I could afford to be a little more selective in my dating process.

The Law of Attraction is an essential foundation to creating your Happily Ever After: it is something for all of us. I shared my methodology while working with my client Carrie and found it an effective tool.

Carrie's Story

Carrie, who much like myself had found herself dating the Village Idiots, was tired of spending time and effort on the dating game and ending up with the same type of guy. We talked about the Law of Attraction and the quality of man she wanted to attract vs. the quality of man she was currently attracting. I encouraged Carrie to make a list of the traits and attributes she wanted in a man. Often I have found that there is a direct correlation between the types of guys we attract and our frustration with dating.

When we were first talking about Carrie's list, I believe her response was, "I don't care as long as he isn't a douche." We laughed, but the reality was, she did care, she cared very much in fact. When we don't prioritize what we want in a relationship, we will be flooded with others who don't know what they want. Most single women looking for a relationship will tell you, it isn't about finding *any* man. It is about finding the right man. If that is truly the case, why do we hesitate to create criteria for our future partner? Lack of faith in the process? Are we so jaded in love that we don't believe our ideal partner exists? There is another underlying factor to why we hesitate to set criteria, and it is intimately linked to our mindset. What if we create a list of criteria and we don't find anyone? This is fear. The best way to tackle fear is to attract more positivity and love into our thoughts and dreams.

I asked Carrie to complete the following questions:

1. **Do I know what characteristics and attributes I want in my Prince?** If yes, make a list. It doesn't have to be perfect, and it isn't set in stone. If no, make a list of the things that you don't want in your Prince, for example, "Not a douche bag" or "Doesn't smoke." Then list the characteristics and attributes in a positive manner. This is a Law of Attraction tool. For example: A non-smoker vs. saying doesn't smoke, kind and loving vs. not a douche bag. The words that we use are important in what we will attract to us.

2. **Will I bring to the relationship the characteristics and attributes that I am looking for in my Prince?** This is an important part of getting ready for the ball. It isn't that we need to be the same person as our Prince, but we need to be realistic in what we are willing to put into the relationship and what we expect to get out of it. For example: If one of the characteristics on our list is to have a man with a rock-hard body, we may need to have a rocking body also, or at least to prioritize health and fitness and eating well. Or perhaps we write on our list that he will text us good morning and goodnight every day. If this is something we value, we must make sure that we are willing to reciprocate it. Probably one of the most important items that people are conflicted with on our list is male/female friendships. We want the guy to be devoted to us, not look or talk to other girls, and yet often times we are not willing to give up our guy friends because we know that they are solidly in the friend zone. We also justify this disparity by believing we know how other wenches think, and therefore our Princes can't be trusted.

3. **What are we bringing to the relationship?** If there are traits or attributes that we are not willing to do or offer, we must take them off our list, or start a personal growth list of items we can work

on with our coach or accountability partner. Bottom line: if you want a Prince, become a Princess.

Look through the list and categorize your wants as Deal Breaker, Likes, and Added Bonuses.

Keep the list handy, revise as needed, and use it as your map through the enchanted forest. Refer to it often, and focus on the positive intentions and vibrations in the list to help draw you to your Prince charming.

Trust the guidance of the list. Sometimes it is easy to get caught up in an interaction with a man, that he may have one or two items on the list, so we forget about the others. Trust the list. Trust that you are worthy and deserving of finding someone who has all of things on the list. Be willing to walk away from anyone who isn't up to standard of the list.

Carrie went forward with her list, and found that she was having much more success. Then she came upon a man she thought might be her Prince. They dated for a few months and things were going well, but then suddenly her Prince revealed himself as a Village Idiot. When Carrie and I met to talk about things, we went back to the list. Did she still have it? Yes, and did he have the required attributes and characteristics, etc.? The answer was no. Sometimes when the hormones kick in, the brain shuts off. Keeping the list handy allows us to notice at the first signs of transformation if our Prince was just an Idiot all along.

In fact, bringing this type of Law of Attraction work into all elements of your life will help you begin to manifest a positive change and lay a foundation for your Happily Ever After.

~ *Chapter 5* ~

Where There Is Smoke, Beware of the Dragon

The Dragon Archetype

Men who belong in this category are masters of illusion, magic, manipulation, and are masters of deception; they confuse you with their smoke and mirrors and they intrigue you with their good looks and smooth words. They present themselves as a Prince, but it is only after the smoke has settled that you realize they are beasts and sorcerers. They have a high-level commitment to the sanctity of the game they play. Similar to the rules of a fight club (one never talks about fight club), so is the credo of the Dragon. You never talk about or admit to the illusion or the game, you move forward steadfastly, and you stay focused on the end result: getting what you want from your victim and leaving her feeling like it was entirely her fault for not being smarter.

It's so easy to get caught up in the excitement and potential of a new relationship that it becomes more about the magic of the illusions and less about the magic of connection. I was guilty of this myself. After all, I knew what I wanted in a relationship. I wanted the Prince, the castle, and the white picket fence around the moat. Finding someone who wanted that also was a little more problematic. The Village Idiots were just looking for a woman, any woman. I knew that I didn't want that, I needed a bit more strategy to my hunt.

I was evolved enough in relationships to know that I couldn't say exactly what I wanted in the first few meetings. That could be overwhelming and intimidating. So unless I was asked a direct question, I didn't answer directly. In truth, even when I was asked directly what I wanted, I tended to be vague about my specific desires because I wanted at least a chance at getting to know the guy better. I thought of it more as a strategic start to a potential relationship, but Dragons are expert strategists and his game of manipulation was more of a challenge than this Lady-in-waiting was prepared for.

The Dragon is quite possibly the most dangerous of all the archetypes. He doesn't want his true form to be revealed, so even if you question his sincerity, he is always there with another distraction to throw you off his trail of deceit. Dragons are in it for the long game; they will present as Sage, Knight, and Prince. For a Dragon, it is about continuing the performance until they get exactly what they want from you.

There were other Dragons in my life, as if being burned the first time should have been lesson enough. It was not. The Dragon Mark was especially skilled in the powers of manipulation and deceit. At one point his rouse so convincing that I even believed we were dating, or at least going to date. We spent our days texting back and forth, talking about life, dreams, etc. Occasionally we would meet each other at different activities with mutual friends. I was even warned by those friends that the Dragon Mark was bad news. I figured that it was just jealousy on their part. I even did a few extra affirmation steps with the Dragon, and asked him about the rumors I had heard. Just as I suspected, there was always a reason. A bitter ex, spreading lies. I knew his ex, and she was crazy. I had heard that he was a player. So I asked about his extra-curricular activities.

He told me that there was a girl. They had an understanding. It was a "friends with benefits" (FWB) agreement. I asked him if I was going to get attacked by this girl in the parking lot if she found out we were talking. He laughed and said no, that their arrangement allowed him to explore other options. I asked him point blank, "Am I a serious option you are exploring, or just someone to get your wiggle on with?" He laughed and said, "Both." Admittedly I didn't love the answer, but the prospect of having a real relationship with him was very enticing. We continued to talk, we even went out on dinner dates, and to the movies. We hadn't specifically addressed becoming exclusive, but in my mind that was just a formality. We had been intimate on several occasions, and the connection and chemistry seemed to be growing. Then one night, the Dragon Mark wanted to come over. My children were home, so it wasn't going to happen. I knew that he was disappointed, but I wasn't willing to introduce him to my children until I knew that we had a serious future together.

The next day I received a notice on social media that he was in a relationship. I was a little shocked and confused. I knew he was disappointed, but how could one night have made such a drastic change in his feelings for me?

Then I started looking through social media. I was an idiot. The relationship notice was dated back to before the Dragon and I had ever even met. I was lied to. I was lied to for months. Even after all the times I had questioned his sincerity, I was still lied to. The Dragon sent me a text message of apology. He said he probably should have talked to me before. Things with his FWB had become more serious. In looking at her profile, she had been in a committed relationship with him for months that appeared to be very serious at least on her part. FML! Not only did the Dragon dupe me, but also he made me the other woman. As he tried to explain away his actions, to rationalize what he had done, he said that he didn't plan it. That "she speaks to my heart in a way that you can't." What the hell does that mean? I countered with "But I speak to your penis?" He laughed and said, "Yes, you do."

Now I was a village idiot. How did I get to this point? I am sorry, get to this point *again*? I was already burned by a Dragon years ago, and just when I thought I was doing better, along comes the Dragon Mark and I am sucked into his illusion also. What was I missing here?

It is easy for each of us to get caught up in our circumstances and get lost in the reasons why we don't deserve to be happy or find happiness, or even why it is that we are not attracting the quality of men we want in our lives. Do we deserve to be punished or lonely forever because we repeatedly have made poor choices in relationships or with men? Depending on how you were raised, you may feel like a higher power rewards those who are faithful, and curses those who are not. But what we learned about with the Law of Attraction is that our thoughts and the energy that we put into the world will dictate whether the Dragons we see before us are going to suck us into their games and distract us with their smoke, or if they are going to drop the games and illusions and show us their true selves. My point being a Dragon is just a dragon, whether he breathes fire or blows smoke, or is honest about his desires with us, his power is derived from our beliefs about him and the energy that we devote to him.

Ultimately I have learned that it wasn't about what happened to me with the Dragons that changed my Happily Ever After. It was that I had a belief about myself that I did not deserve the fairytale ending, because of my poor choices or that I was an idiot. I think this is also what held me back in my own marriage. I had a decent guy, he loved me as best that he knew how to love me, and yet in the end it was my beliefs about wanting so much more that ended that story also.

If our destiny is created by our thoughts and our beliefs, we need to stay aware of the things that we ask for and dream about, what we attract to us through the Law of Attraction, as it will set the foundation for what we will receive. The key of the Dragon Archetype is this: I am a powerful agent for change. I am responsible for manifesting goals and setting boundaries to keep me on track. I want to make sure that I am manifesting those things that will help me reach my Happily Ever After and move through the frustration and negativity quickly.

Manifesting and Setting Boundaries

The basic steps to manifesting are these:

☐ What do you believe? Try this thought: I am deserving of a fairytale relationship full of romance and Happily Ever After.

☐ What is it you desire? In addition to thinking about your beliefs, you have to be willing to *ask* for what you want. You may say, "I want to have a dream come true life." Great, don't we all? But what does a dream come true life look like for you? If you were guaranteed to get exactly what you want, what specifically would you ask for?

☐ What are your intentions? More specifically, what is it you intend to do in this Happily Ever After? Once you achieve this Happily Ever After, how will your life be different? This is where the context around your dream comes into play. Is this truly what you want, and will it accomplish what you desire?

☐ Do you have the passion? Passion is the key ingredient in manifesting. It is the secret ingredient in the magic potion. Does what you want align with your heart? Is this something that you are willing to work tirelessly on to have in your life? There are a lot of resources that you can use or help rely on to assist you through the manifesting process, but if you are not passionate about your outcome, nothing can help you truly achieve it.

As we begin to move forward with manifesting our dreams, we realize the importance of setting boundaries for ourselves and others around us. We can't create a new life, a new dream, or a new relationship if we continue through the same path in the woods that we have always taken. It isn't easy to change, but it is impossible to change if we try to stay the same person. If you are truly passionate about manifesting love in your life, you will be willing to let go of beliefs, relationships, and/or dramas that are preventing you from moving forward. Setting boundaries allows you to hold a sacred space for you to change, create, and find that Happily Ever After. Setting boundaries is also a place where we honor the change process. This is a place where we get easily side tracked, or perhaps caught up in the bright and shiny new toy or relationship. It's important to set our boundaries, and to hold them.

My client Jo worked with me on manifesting during one of my six-week women's wellness classes. We talked about boundaries and the importance of focusing on our goals and staying on track to achieve them. Jo had met a guy through online dating who was a great conversationalist. He seemed to be very interested and attentive to Jo's needs. After about a month, she started to notice that he was very good at redirecting the conversation and saying all the right things. Jo realized that she had a smoke-blowing dragon on her hands. It is one thing to notice that there may be an issue, but if you have been desperately seeking love, you may not be ready to kick him out of the picture for being a smoker. Jo continued to see him, only paying closer attention to her manifesting and holding her boundaries.

The demise of her dragon came one day when he wanted to make Jo a nice dinner at her house. She was excited, and as he talked about the menu for the evening, he mentioned that he would be frying catfish. Jo doesn't eat catfish. Honestly, this wasn't the first time that the discussion of catfish had come up in their relationship. She told the dragon that no, she was not interested in him making catfish, let alone in her kitchen in her house. The smell of fried fish is something that lingers for days, not to mention, Jo was very clear about not wanting catfish. The dragon said, fine, he would come up with something else.

When the big night arrived, Jo had to stay late at work, so the dragon started making dinner before she got home. When she pulled into the driveway, she could smell dinner cooking. What was he making? Deep fried catfish! Why? Because he had no respect for Jo's boundaries or desires. This was all about meeting his needs. I am proud of Jo! When she entered the house and confirmed his blatant disrespect for her, she threw the dragon out. She held to her boundaries, and chose to honor herself rather than tolerate being disrespected.

Ladies, it does no good for us to try to make changes in our lives if we continue to put up with the same crap we always have and maintain the same behavior that got us in the situation to begin with.

We have the ability to create our new story, and the beauty of it is, if we start a story we don't like, we can change it! But start it we must. If we have been playing the part of the evil or bitter queen and have been in a negative mindset for a long time, we won't automatically become Snow White overnight. Law of Attraction and Manifesting take practice.

Manifesting Exercise:

1. We must ask ourselves "What do I want in my life?" If we don't know the answer to this make a list of the things that we don't want in our life and go from there. For example, we don't want to date any dragons, beggars, or peasants.

2. Create a positive Law of Attraction statement with our goal. Change out any negatives like don't, can't, won't, etc. and flip the statement for what we would rather have instead. "I want to date good guys."

3. Review your statement, the goal is to create one relationship statement and make it full and juicy. Take out words like "want," "can," "will," and "need," things that give you an opportunity to do it at a later time, or leave our goal to "wanting or needing." The best method is to state it in first person as if it has already come to fruition: "I attract and date, honest, caring, positive, supportive, true princely men."

4. Set intentions: this is where we make our plans. How will our lives be different once we have achieved our goal? There will be more romance, companionship, and passion. What will be gained by us attracting and dating high quality men? What type of personal growth or changes do we need to make to attract high quality men?

5. Infuse passion into the plan. Passion allows for a dash of magic along with our measure of commitment to achieving our goals. Make some action plans and start taking action, maybe by revising our dating profiles, maybe by deleting

them from a site altogether. Creating small action steps imbued with intention helps us achieve our goals and manifest our Happily Ever After.

6. Set boundaries! It is always easier to set our limits before we are tested on them. Sometimes in the heat of the moment we are tempted to push our limits, perhaps to avoid the smoke in the lair.

    a. Set boundaries that honor us and are honor our dream come true.

    b. Always know our worth and that no matter what we have done previously, we are deserving and worthy of accomplishing our dreams.

    c. When we feel our boundaries or goals may be at risk, allow ourselves to say "No" sooner, and feel no remorse for honoring our desires. Allow ourselves time to think before we say "Yes" to make sure that our choices are in alignment with our overall goal to guarantee successful manifestation and achievement of our Happily Ever After.

Chapter 6

Where Is the Knight in Shining Armor to Save this Damsel in Distress?

I may have mentioned before that I am a hopeless romantic. I love "love"! I love the fairytale, and I love the idea of the Knight in Shining Armor swooping in to save the damsel in distress. That is probably why the Knight in Shining Armor Archetype is by far my favorite of all. They are easy to love and provide almost every element a Lady-in-waiting could want in a fairytale romance. The challenge that this archetype poses is that in order to have a Knight in Shining Armor save you, you have to need to be saved or be broken. And there's a catch: when you are out of imminent danger, the Knight in Shining Armor will return to his search for his own holy grail. Staying broken or in distress is counterintuitive to the advice given in previous chapters about like attracting like and manifesting the outcome you desire. Careful, ladies. If you want to be saved, you have to wait in danger.

Before I understood the Law of Attraction and manifesting, I met a Knight in Shining Armor. I knew that he was there to save me, because on the morning that we met I had considered suicide. I was still married and I had truly forgotten who I was, what my value was, and whether I made a difference in this world. I felt as though the mistakes of my past had consumed my light and that I would never have my fairytale. I was tempted as I drove to work to cross over the centerline into oncoming traffic. How easy it would have been to end it all! Then the thought of my children came to my mind; they would never understand. Their lives would never be the same, and although I had screwed up a lot in my life, I was still a pretty good mom. My children were the only people that I recognized loved me.

I pulled off the road at that moment and prayed, "God, help me!" Then I sat as tears and mascara ran down my face. It was approximately 20 minutes before the sobbing subsided and I could successfully navigate my way to work. When I got to work, I had meetings throughout the day. In one of those meetings, I met a true Knight in Shining Armor, Tim Grant. I will never forget his first words to me. He said, "Stripper shoes! Nice!" He most definitely made an impression on me that day, and I couldn't be offended because my shoes did look a little like stripper shoes, but more subtle, and they were on sale for $8.00.

Whether it was a blessing from God or a gift from my Fairy Godparents, Tim had arrived in my life at a time when I so desperately needed some support and guidance. I am almost certain he had no idea at that moment what was about to happen, and yet the magic just flowed. I was looking for someone to save me. Tim was looking for something too, and I was the girl for him. We became friends. Just friends. He was strong, noble, and honest. Sometimes painfully honest. Tim wasn't interested in me for any other reason than to be a friend. That was exactly what I needed. Tim was the Knight who told me that I was living exactly the life I wanted to live or else I would change it. He never accepted my excuses for not moving forward or making progress in my life. More than anything, he made me accountable for my life, my decisions, and my path. His favorite phrases were, "It is what it is," and "Do it or don't, it doesn't matter to me."

Oh, how I hated those words! All I wanted was to be of value to someone, and he would repeatedly deny me the satisfaction of living my life for him. He didn't want that responsibility. He forced me to step up and take control of my life again. Through my separation and divorce, Tim continued to be my lifeline. He helped me find counseling that worked for me. He was also on his own journey to find the holy grail of happiness and overcome the challenges in his life, and I like to think that he needed a friend as much as I needed one.

After my divorce, it was very easy for me to let my hopeless romantic go and do all of the crazy things that Ladies-in-waiting do when they think they are in love. There was no doubt that over time we had grown to love each other, but there is a fundamental difference between falling in love with someone and loving someone. My Knight in Shining Armor didn't love me that way. I was devastated. We had probably the most functional adult relationship I had ever had in my life, and yet to him, I was just a friend. This is not how the fairytale ends! The Knight in Shining Armor swoops in, saves the damsel in distress, and they ride off into the sunset and live Happily Ever After. At no part in any fairytale does the Lady-in-waiting end up in the friend zone.

I tried really hard to convince him that we had something awesome. I got tired of hearing things like, "You are awesome, but…" or "Of course I love you, I just don't see you that way." I was hurt. I thought about all the conversations we'd had, all the times that we were there for each other. If that wasn't the fairytale ending, I didn't know what was. Needless to say, things got a bit tense for us. Clarification: *I* made things tense between us by not respecting his feelings towards me. At one point we had a fight over something small, and Tim was gone. Even though I felt my dreams were crumbling, I was strong and I was not going to let this stop me. I mean, I had been dating guys because I was obsessed with finding a relationship. Maybe I figured, somewhere in my craziness, that I would date a few rebound guys, and then maybe, just maybe things would work out with Tim. The fairytale was falling apart and I wasn't sure I could function without him. Until I did.

I learned a lot from Tim, and a lot about myself when I no longer had the Knight in Shining Armor to protect me. I learned that no matter how much we want something in life, we can't manifest for other people. I learned that by setting expectations of how my story with Tim would end, I missed a lot of magic and opportunities for other good things in my life. I learned that there is an important balance between giving and receiving that must be maintained. I also learned that I had to have my own thing going on, otherwise, I was going to be lost again. I also learned a few things about the psyche of men that truly go against everything women have been taught about how men think. I have had to learn and relearn this lesson many times, as it is easy one to get caught up in the tale of the Knight in Shining Armor archetype. It is wonderful to be rescued as a Lady-in-waiting, but that isn't the fairytale. However, the key given by the Knights in Shining Armor archetype unlocks valuable lessons, and taking the following actions will help create that Happily Ever After.

You Can't Manifest for Someone Else

Wouldn't it be great if we could just wish upon a star and make it happen? As much as I hate to admit it, I probably spent a solid year after my separation wishing on stars, eyelashes, and coins in fountains that Tim would fall in love with me the way I thought I fell for him. It doesn't work that way. At one point, I even went to a psychic to see what she saw in my future relationship with him. Her response was, "It is what it is!" As annoying as that was, it was also an excellent validation of her insight. She continued on to talk about free will and the importance that our choices make in our lives. We can't manifest our specific desires for another person, because that may interfere with their free choice and free will to decide their own destiny. It made sense; my religious youth had taught me that free choice is a God-given gift. Sometimes the Knights in Shining Armor are in our life for a reason or a season to help guide us to become the best versions of ourselves and help us move to a place where we can create our dream come true. It is our job to love them, learn from them, and let them leave.

Releasing Expectations

As a hopeless romantic, I sometimes used to start planning the fairytale wedding and the castle with the white picket fence right when I met someone and before I even recognized what, if any, part we may play in each other's lives. I have learned that when I create expectations for the outcome, more often than not my soon-to-be Knight in Shining Armor will be running for the hills or falling on his sword to end the relationship. When it comes to achieving our goals, we need to set our intentions but also allow ourselves to be open and curious about how it is going to be achieved. If we are busy trying to control every aspect of a relationship, not only is it stressful and exhausting, it's counter-productive. We find ourselves in analysis paralysis, where we are thinking and planning but afraid to execute because we are unsure how we can guarantee our outcome. Although it seems counterintuitive, sometimes it is better to set goals, release expectations, and trust that as long as you are working towards your goal, you will be on the right path. Most importantly, when it comes to expectations, is everyone on the same page? No matter what we think a guy's actions are, if his words say, "I am not that into you," believe him!

Balance Giving and Receiving

This is often difficult for the relationship-obsessed or the hopeless romantic, because we are in it to win it, so we willingly devote hours to making our relationship successful. This is not only true with the Knights in Shining Armor, but also with the Beggars, Peasants, and Dragons also. We give and give, and then find ourselves frustrated if our expectations are not being met. In some cases it can make us crazy. Balance giving and receiving in the relationship. It can be in the little things like, is there equal contribution of time, effort, finances, etc. or is it all being handled by one of you? Do you have a clear understanding of what this relationship means to all involved parties?

It is also important that we learn to give without expectation. My client Cheri struggled with this, especially at the holidays. Her boyfriend Luke was not really into celebrating, and Cheri was frustrated because every year she spent more money than she should have to make sure Luke had a great Christmas, buying him whatever was on his list. Then, on Christmas, she was always disappointed to see that where she had purchased him an iPad, he had bought her a $25 iTunes card.

It wasn't that Luke was a cheap jerk. Luke didn't see the point in overspending on holidays, but throughout the year he would buy Cheri gifts for no reason at all: a bracelet from a bonus check he got at work, or flowers because she was having a bad day. Cheri's issue wasn't Luke; it was that she was giving with the expectation of receiving in return. If I do this, you should do this. Also equating his commitment to the relationship based on the gift given at Christmas. This was a belief that we worked on with Cheri, to give without expectation. The counter of that was to receive without obligation. At times we get so caught up in this imaginary score card that we forget to allow people to do nice things for us, and just be grateful.

Have Your Own Thing Going On

In the relationship coaching business, I have had opportunities to talk at length with men about what it is that they most want in a woman. I have also, through many failed attempts with some Knights in Shining Armor, been given similar feedback. Please listen, as this is very important: Real confidence is sexy. Being successful in our own life, having our own goals, being a whole and complete person with or without a romantic relationship, is sexy. We will delve into this more in the next chapter, but the harsh reality is, more often than not, that men looking for real relationships are attracted to the whole package: body, mind, and soul. If we don't know what our "thing" is? Don't worry. What better to manifest in our life than our own "thing?"

For me, it was intuitive life coaching. I mentioned that Tim had helped me find some counseling. It wasn't conventional counseling. I tried that, but I wasn't content to talk about my issues session after session with little to no results – remember I already had a perfect support system of friends I could commiserate with, and I was trying to break that habit. I started working with a beautiful woman named Tanya. She was a PSYCH® facilitator. PSYCH® is a form of energy work, a change modality that helped me to shift the outdated beliefs that I had, deal with some traumatic events in my life, and truly begin to heal to create the fairytale ending I desired. Through working with Tanya, I fell in love with energy work. It opened the door for me to healing and manifesting in my life, not just relationships, but in all aspects of my life. I worked with Tanya for about a year, and she encouraged me to take the classes myself and become a PSYCH® facilitator also.

It was through this program that I found my love for helping and healing others. It became my "thing." Regardless if that makes me more attractive to men or not, I can tell you that having my own "thing" has definitely made my life more attractive to me. No longer am I a girl who wonders if she is valuable or important to others. I receive daily affirmations that my life makes a difference. I am worthwhile, and the passion that fills my life now is life-supporting and life-sustaining. I am whole.

Chapter 7
Unlocking the Magic of Self- Love Through Failed Relationships

Oliver Wendell Holmes has a few insightful words to say about expanding our minds: "A mind, once expanded by a new idea, never returns to its original dimensions."

The same is true for our hearts. Once our heart has expanded, it, too, will never return to its original size. Even in the most tragic of heartbreaks, the heart will heal and the cracks will mend, and we will always know what it is like to have loved and have grown in a relationship. When we look back at some of the most crushing break-ups, we see that they are the ones that give us the most growth and guidance to move forward in our lives. To this day, I look back to my first true love and see that even though we were just in high school, he unknowingly set the bar for so many of the relationships I would have going forward in my life. I experienced some other devastating departures, and obviously not from the Dragons whose goals were always ill-intended. The most devastating were those of the Knights in Shining Armor that amounted to only friendships. It was the separation from the ones I thought of as soul mates, the ones I would always have in my life, that were the most devastating.

When Tim and I had our big argument, it was over something stupid, something minor. Then he vanished overnight. I was hurt – no, I was crushed – but I had no choice but to survive and keep moving forward. It was painful and annoying, but now in hindsight I can see that I became reliant on his wisdom and guidance to define who I was. I was using him as a crutch, constantly seeking affirmation that all would be well. I wasn't taking responsibility for my journey or my path. I was chasing the fluffy bunnies and rainbows of affirmations, but was slow to do the actual work. I unknowingly put too much pressure on him. My optimism became a curse. Although our initial argument was over a birthday dinner, I wouldn't find out until almost a year later that the wedge between us was caused by my lack of respect and not honoring where Tim was on his journey. He wasn't in a place where he could just hope for the best. We ultimately had different perspectives on the path to healing.

In that year away from Tim, I became stronger each day. I met new and wonderful people who I never would have met had I stayed so reliant on Tim for his advice. Our time apart allowed me to learn and grow and become more in tune with my spiritual gifts and intuition. During that time of growth, I dreamed and prayed that Tim and I would find our way back to each other. It wasn't until we could learn to agree to disagree about the path to healing, and be grateful that we were both working towards our goals, that we could be friends and confidants again. I doubt Tim and I will ever get back to the level of dependency we had on one another. Truth be told, that in itself is a testament to the amount of growth and healing we have experienced. Loving someone enough to let your relationship evolve, even if it means letting go, allows you to feel the beauty of the connection when your paths cross again. It is nice to know you have a Knight in Shining Armor a phone call away. It is also empowering to know that you can rescue yourself. This break -up taught me that I was strong and capable of being the hero in my own life.

I had just completed my training in the Advanced PSYCH® facilitator program. In this class, you begin to do higher-level energy work and healing. I had also began to practice my new spirituality by focusing more on prayer and meditation, as well as using crystals, essential oils, and energy clearing tactics to help me move forward from the break-up with Tim and get my own thing going on.

I met Johnny during my hiatus away from Tim. He was more than a Knight in Shining Armor. He was magic! He came into my life for such a brief moment, but the impact he would make would forever alter the course of my life and the lives of those around me.

I met Johnny and his girlfriend through softball. They were new to town, and I was immediately drawn to them. They were fun! They had a different perspective on life. Johnny and his girlfriend were very open and curious about energy work. In fact, they were probably the first of my softball friends that understood me.

I remember one particular week when I was struggling. I was still trying to find my Prince Charming, only this time, I was working all the angles – energy work, meditation, manifestation, etc. – I was bound and determined to manifest a relationship with my friend Cody, the personal trainer. I was passionate about it. I don't know if Cody knew that I had planned out our whole fairytale ending or not, but I was moving forward to manifesting it. I was confident that this would be the one. This was the Prince Charming who would make me forget all of the others before him. Only I forgot. Relationships are about free choice, and you can't manifest something for someone else. Naturally I was frustrated when things weren't progressing with the trainer.

Then a train wreck happened. Cody started to reconcile with his ex-girlfriend. This wasn't in my plan. Suddenly, they were a couple again. To make it worse, his ex made sure that he cut all ties with any of his female friends who weren't also her friends. I felt like this was my shot at having it all, and he didn't even give us a real chance. I knew that I could have been his Happily Ever After. In my devastation and frustration, I began to ask for some signs or affirmations from the Universe that things were going to work out for me. I went to a gong meditation, and while I was there, I received a strong message that things were going to be just fine. I also received a heavy dose of reminding me that my gifts and intuition are not to be self-serving, that I couldn't manifest for others. I wasn't sure that was sign enough or that I would recover unscathed from the loss of Cody.

Then I went to Johnny's birthday celebration. We met at a local bar for games and drinks. I was always the designated driver, which is something from my Mormon upbringing that has always stayed with me. Stay safe, stay sober! Johnny on the other hand, was far from sober. He came over to talk to me and just wanted to make sure I knew my life was good. If you have ever had a conversation with someone who is thoroughly drunk, you will know that often passion and repetition are abundant. Johnny kept telling me, "Life is good! You know?" The extent of his elaboration was to say, "Your life is good, your kids are good, your life is good, only good things are coming your way, life is good." Strangely I felt that this was in fact an answer to my prayers. This too shall pass, and he was right. My life was good.

The next day after Johnny had sobered up, I thanked him for his words of wisdom, and told him he was an answer to my prayer. I told him that he probably didn't even know how divinely timed his message was, but that he was definitely a conduit for my answered prayer.

Johnny laughed. He said that he actually did know that he was an answer to my prayer, and to the prayers of many others. Johnny wasn't bragging about it. He just had great intuition and connection with his spiritual gifts. Johnny and I talked more openly about our intuition and energy work. He was a wonderful mentor to help me understand some of the things I was going through.

Johnny and his girl broke-up, and she asked if I could talk to him. He wanted to move back to Montana to be closer to his children, plus things weren't really working out for him here. As I talked to Johnny, we began to share our goals and dreams for what we wanted to contribute to the world. It was almost startling: my big dream, number 18 on my list of things to manifest, was in perfect alignment with Johnny's big dreams.

Unfortunately Johnny moved back to Montana, but he and I had forged a connection that I thought most assuredly would last an eternity. We helped each other find ourselves. I could think of calling him and my phone would ring. There was so much magic in our connection. Even knowing that he was a Knight in Shining Armor and I shouldn't fall for him, I did. The romantic in me likes to run to the edge of love and jump. I fell for him. I fell for him hard. There was such a crazy connection between us I could literally place my hand on his and feel what was going on inside his mind and heart. Connections like that don't come around often; I felt that there was awesome potential there. This was magic.

I wasn't in a rush to move forward. He was still healing from his break-up with his girlfriend. She and I were no longer friends. Johnny and I had opportunities to escalate our relationship to a new level, but didn't. What we had was already like gold, I didn't want to mess it up. We were working on creating a dream. A dream that could heal the world. I loved, loved, loved this man. He got me. He understood all of my weirdness; he saluted me and respected me when I let my freak flag fly and tell him about the crazy things happening in my life. We were making plans for joint family vacations and spending Christmas together.

I couldn't imagine a life without Johnny until it happened. It could have been the stress and guilt he felt from his break-up, it could have been that he was overwhelmed by the connection we had, it could have been that he didn't see me as a romantic possibility. Maybe there was just too much to feel when we were together. Whatever his reasoning was, I would never find out. He asked for some time and space to figure some things out. He called once or twice after that, to get a few answers to questions. You see, I was his oracle. If you believe in psychics, you might understand what I mean when I say that I had a direct line into Johnny's pure potentiality.

It has been years, and I have not heard from or seen Johnny. I will occasionally send an email to him, or a random text message. I don't ask for anything, I only send good thoughts of vibrations his way. As painful as it was to lose him, the growth, support, and connection with him for those eight months gave me a lifetime of love, insights, and courage to embrace my newfound gifts. Through Johnny leaving, I learned what real love is. I learned to love myself. I learned that I had enough love for both of us, and that I could let him go without hate, anger, or malice. Johnny fundamentally changed what love and loving relationships meant to me.

The Foundation for Happily Ever After

As I was working through things after Johnny left, I received a download, or message, about what real love is. There is something about our human experience that takes some of the simplest concepts and screws them up when we apply them. My whole life, I had been chasing this fairytale dream of True Love: finding my Prince, my Knight is Shining Armor who would love me and accept me unconditionally in my life. Through that unconditional love from a partner, I thought, I would finally have my Happily Ever After. Johnny taught me when we have tasted the sweet nectar of connection, a soul mate connection, it is so magical it opens up our heart and transforms the essence of who we are. In fact, it transforms us so much that even if or when that soul mate moves on, we can never return to the person we were before them. We have been changed for good. We know love. We experienced a love so strong and so pure that we fell head-over-heels for ourselves.

We love ourselves so unconditionally that we embrace all of the crazy, wonderful, sometimes shameful things in we did in our past. We love ourselves so passionately that we emerge, whole and complete. We are able to embrace everything beautiful and miserable that has happened in our life and make it all part of our authentic self. The things that I learned from Johnny about love set the bar for every relationship that will come after. When we have this radical self-love as our foundation, then and only then can we create our dream come true. A passion-filled life based on anything other than this radical self-love will eventually crumble. Princes will reveal themselves as Frogs, Dragons, or Idiots and Knights in Shining Armor will leave.

Chapter 8

Don't Be Fooled by the Frog Prince

As we evolve and continue to make changes in our lives, we see that the quality of the men we attract also evolves. The good news, as we begin to heal, is that we will attract fewer of the Knight in Shining Armor types and spare our hearts from being rescued. We will not be tempted by or attracted to the Village Idiots. We have learned to recognize the smoke and can walk away before we get burned by the Dragon. Unfortunately, there is also bad news: no matter how together we feel, we will never be so attractive and put-together that the Idiots won't hit on us. As we set and achieve goals and become a force to be reckoned with, we begin to gain confidence – real confidence, the sexy, hot confidence that will be noticed throughout the Kingdom.

I remember when I finally decided that I was a Princess and ready to go to the ball. I had been focused more on my coaching business, teaching evening classes, etc. I felt I was ready to move forward and start dating again. It didn't take long – that's what happens when you are a Princess. The Kingdom responds quickly. When Josh and I met, he had many of the Princely characteristics I was looking for, but he was still a bit rough around the edges. We began talking and going out often. I remember how easily he could make me laugh, how nice it was to be with him. He was smart, he was strong, he was opinionated, and he had a smile that could stop me in my tracks. It didn't take long for this self-evolved Princess to fall head-over-heels for this Prince, and quickly.

Admittedly I was more into him than he was into me in the beginning. I was blinded by the honeymoon phase of the new relationship, and I didn't see what was happening. I didn't realize it at the time, but he wasn't my Prince. He was a Frog Prince. He stole my heart, by talking the good relationship talk. He welcomed my affection – he loved to hug, kiss, and cuddle. He desired my attention – we would talk of the phone for hours, or just watch Netflix. But he still left me wanting quality time versus quantity of time. He left me hoping for a chance to share my world with him versus me just being absorbed into his. He left me wishing for something more.

Although I knew that I desperately needed to continue focusing on my coaching business, I found myself being distracted by the Frog Prince. All of the manifesting practices that I had put into place, like meditation and journaling, were slipping away from me. I could feel the shift in myself, but didn't recognize what it was because I was losing myself again in the quest for a relationship. As things began to shift, I became frustrated and impatient.

When I would try to talk to the Frog Prince about my feelings, he would correct me, and tell me about the world according to him. He perceived me very differently than I perceived myself. I saw myself as a strong, confident, beautiful, smart, relaxed Princess who was contributing to a successful relationship. He saw me as jealous, insecure, and less intelligent. He would follow his comments with things like, "But don't worry, you can work on that, overall I think you are awesome." It would infuriate me! I knew I was awesome! I also knew that in my core, I was not the woman that he perceived. We began disagreeing over the smallest things, and then arguing over even more ridiculous topics.

I was fighting to save a relationship where I was not respected or honored for my gifts and who I was as a person, and more importantly, I didn't want to be there anymore. Why was I doing this? Was it the time I had invested in the relationship? Maybe it was because when we had a good night (it was an amazing night), and it made the bad nights almost disappear. Maybe I was just trying to make my relationship fairytale-worthy.

Was I in love with the thought of being in love, again? Had I jumped into this before my Princess transformation was fully complete? I was caught up in the newness and hormones of the situation that I failed to see that there was not a real connection or respect. How did I get here? More importantly why was I still here?

I ended it immediately with Josh. If this was a test to see if I was worthy of new Princess life, I almost failed. Or had I? This was, after all, a different archetype, and a different relationship than the others. It appeared as though this was the final key to unlocking my relationship potential.

This ladies, is when we are put to the test. This is the time when we must decide, are we ready for the ball? We have been manifesting, and working with the Law of Attraction and setting healthy boundaries. We have shifted our mindset from finding any man to finding the right type of man. We have committed to being the hero of our own story instead of waiting to be rescued. We have raised the bar for love and what we are willing to accept. Our transformation is complete. We have become the Princess and are ready to attract our Prince. Here is where we meet the Frog Prince Archetype.

The Frog Prince Archetype

Frog Princes are mostly just frogs who stop evolving before they turn into a Prince. They present themselves as a male version of Mary Poppins: "Practically Perfect in Every Way." They are incredibly close to our dream-come-true, and often present as the potential "one." In fact they can be so close to our Prince ideal that they have us believing that if they made just a few small changes, they would be the perfect Prince. Maybe if we just invest a little more time in the relationship, they will change!

No. That perfection will always elude us. Frogs don't become Princes just because a Princess wants them to change. In fact, the only way a frog will become a Prince is if he wants to change for himself. Don't get caught up in the idea of changing your frog into a Prince. It won't happen, and the frogs, well, they can't even carry a glass slipper, so they generally aren't prepared for the ball either. But the key that the Frog Prince gives to us is the necessity and power that lies behind making minor adjustments that result in major change. Breaking up with Josh was a minor change that made a major adjustment to my life. If the Kingdom was testing my commitment to staying a Princess and not returning to old habits, I was up for the challenge. I was no longer a Lady-in-waiting. I had goals and boundaries, I had forged incredible relationships, I loved myself unconditionally, and I resolved that I would never be in a relationship in which I was not honored and respected again. Another minor adjustment that I needed to make was to ensure that I will be received with the respect and grace that a Princess deserves. But how does this happen?

> "You teach people how to treat you by what you allow,
> what you stop, and what you reinforce."
> **TONY GASKINS**

We teach people how to treat us. If we want to be respected, we must be respectful of ourselves and hold those boundaries that we have created to allow us a safe or sacred space to evolve. Men are simple creatures. If you want them to understand the importance of romance in your relationship, romance yourself. Buy flowers for yourself, light candles for dinner, or take a romantic bubble bath. Buy your favorite chocolates for special occasions. If you have a self-care process, like meditation, journaling, spa treatments, Girls' Night Out, etc., share your process with your partner and the value you get from it. Invite them to join you on occasion, but never postpone your self-care to care for someone else. Show them that you honor and appreciate yourself, and soon they will follow suit (aka lead by example).

> "Perhaps we should love ourselves so fiercely, that when others see us they know exactly how it should be done."
> **RUDY FRANCISCO**

Create passion in all elements of your life: career, home, family, and relationships. Strive to feel whole and complete at all times on your own, regardless of the circumstances.

Don't be afraid to kiss a few frogs while you practice dating, but don't make them your pets. Be ready, willing, and able to walk away from any situation that does not meet your highest and best good.

Trust your gut, your intuition, and remember that you are worth having exactly the kind of relationship and life you desire. Don't settle for less than your Dream Come True.

Minor Adjustments for Major Change:

1. Be honest with yourself: Is this experience in alignment with my Dream Come True? Does it contribute to success in all facets of my life?

2. Be accountable. What steps do I need to take to maximize my potential and realign with my goals? Is this something that is within my power to change?

Trust your intuition and discernment. The greatest gift we can give to ourselves is to *trust* our own decision-making *through self-respect*. We can't make anyone respect us, but we can always honor and respect ourselves.

Chapter 9

When You Run Out of Fairy Dust

It is easy when we start something new to give it 110% - especially when we see immediate results or get a taste of the instant gratification. We want a quick fix, a magic pill to fast forward us to the point in our life where we have already fixed our problem and are living our dream come true.

Cami has been a dear friend and client for many years. As we began working through the different elements of creating our fairytale ending, Cami was feeling empowered. She had a vision and direction of what she wanted to accomplish in her life. Cami was ready to move forward and get ready for the ball. She had begun to investigate new hobbies like painting, crafts, and redecorating her home to create a sacred space for her to grow.

As she was working on her transition, an ex-fiancé contacted her. This was a man who she had loved and wanted to marry. Cami was feeling the buzz of empowerment, and so she felt comfortable talking to and opening up the door for conversations and to investigate the potential with her ex. After all, she had made changes in her life, and he said that he had changed also. With her newfound confidence, Cami began to engage more with him. They were texting and talking daily. She had been upfront and honest with him about who she was, and the changes she had made in her life. He was very supportive of them, and was eager for an opportunity to possibly pick up where they left off.

But weeks turned into months, and the previous struggles they had had in their relationship were still there. Not to mention that there were new levels of frustration that were beginning to form. This was someone that Cami had invested years of her life with. But as she had become more aware and enlightened about her role and responsibility in the relationship, especially when it came to being responsible for her own happiness, she realized that he was not on the same page with her relationship goals. It was frustrating; here she was trying to make personal progress, and once again, she found herself back at the old Cami, not even wanting to get out of bed. This time it was worse, because her awareness of her progress, empowerment, and having achieved some successes only reinforced that she was not where she needed to be to live her Happily Ever After.

Why did this happen to Cami? She got caught up in life happening and lost focus. It's common and human. We get a taste of success, and then we transition into celebratory mode before we finished all of our work, only to find ourselves months later, back in the same place we were before we started our journey.

Good news: this happens to the best of us. I have experienced this. On-again-off-again relationships with the Frog Prince and PappaBear69 continued to plague my text messages for almost a year. Even the Dragon came back into my life with a new illusion that ended, once again, with another girl earning his heart.

Why does this continue to happen, we ask? Are we gluttons for punishment? It is too hard to release the drama of our past and step off the emotional roller coaster? It is a rarity that we are given the luxury of focusing on only one task or project at a time. We are holistic by nature, and have many facets of our lives all needing daily time and attention. Ultimately the goal for each of us must be to become the best version of ourselves in all facets of life. The bad news is that when we are faced with the challenges, much like Cami, we become acutely aware of what success could be, and that we are failing. We judge ourselves harshly, or commit to an outcome regardless of whether it's an outcome we even desire anymore. Sometimes we need help to navigate the disenchanted forest and help us find the crown of self-love, which can never be damaged, stolen, or lost.

~ *Chapter 10* ~

Becoming the Queen of Hearts

I spent a significant amount of my life chasing Prince Charming and the fairytale ending. I have wasted time in the wrong relationships, hoping that I could transform them into the fantasy relationship of my dreams. I have sent Knights in Shining Armor running for the hills, because I couldn't get over my desire to be with them for Happily Ever After regardless of their feelings for me. I have sought direction and love through mystics and psychics, and failed to see that I have always had the power within myself to manifest all things. I have sacrificed my heart many times over to the Dragons and the Village Idiots, hoping and waiting to find love and happiness. I have kissed dozens of frogs hoping that a magic spark will ignite, and they will turn into my Prince.

If my journey were to be measured based only on the criteria of whether I found my Prince or not, I most definitely would be a failure. I clearly found little to no success in the romance department. But what I did find was this: each time I began to be overly focused or obsessed with dating, I found a new archetype of men. Men that would teach me valuable lessons about finding real love and passion in my life. I found that I am a gifted intuitive, and I have a passion and desire for coaching others who like me are struggling to create their dream-come-true life. I have started my own business, authored a book (and have another on the way), I have found joy and love in the connections I have made. I enjoy karaoke, playing softball, and going to concerts. I love to hike and relax at the lake and enjoy my life. I have served as the Booster Club President and team mom for my children's activities, I have traveled as a chaperone, and grown the relationship between my children and me. All passion-filled ventures and labors of love.

Tim and I are best friends, and I will always value and appreciate his insight into my path. I have forged friendships with some loyal knights – Derek, Jeff, Anthony, Jim, and Nick – who watch out for me and my children, kill spiders, and occasionally provide a shoulder to cry on. I have a beautiful court of Ladies-in-waiting and Princesses who, like me, are transitioning into their own Queendom. When I became disenchanted with finding my Prince Charming, I redefined what Happily Ever After meant for me, and I became not just a Princess, but finally a true and autonomous Queen.

I will forever be grateful to the Archetypes, for without them I would have never found my life's work.

The Six Magic Keys to Unlocking Your Relationship Potential

Are We Ready for the Ball? Are we willing to do the work required to accomplish our dreams?

Mirror Mirror on the Wall, Why in Relationships Do I Stumble and Fall: The basics of law of attraction. Are we watching our thoughts and focusing on the positive outcomes in all areas of our lives? Have we truly detached from the drama and are we consistently making good choices to become the best version of ourselves?

Where There Is Smoke, Beware of the Dragon: Are we actively setting goals and practicing manifestation in all aspects of our lives? Are we creating a positive, loving, and sacred space for us to learn and grow?

Where is the Knight in Shining Armor to Save This Damsel in Distress?: Are we grateful for the opportunities and people who come into our lives to help us learn and grow? Are we able to release control and allow the magic of the Universe to guide our path?

Unlocking the Magic of Self-Love Through Failed Relationships: Are we being gentle with ourselves? Have we forgiven ourselves and others and allowed time for healing? Are we grateful for those who have come and gone in our life for the lessons they have taught us? Are we evolving, moving forward, with our eyes opened? Have we learned to love ourselves and find passion and happiness in all elements of our lives?

Don't Be Fooled by the Frog Prince: Are we accepting only those relationships that respect and honor us as the Divine Royalty we are? Are we making adjustments quickly and rebounding as soon as we realize we are not in alignment with our goals and purpose?

If we were to measure success by whether we defined our own Happily Ever After instead of getting stuck in the outdated belief that Prince Charming is the only fairytale ending, we will find that we have achieved our Dream Come True. As it turns out, Happily Ever After has nothing to do with finding the Prince. It is about getting ready for the ball and building our kingdom with self-love, about manifesting a passion-filled life with meaning and purpose. In the end, the Prince is going to have to get his own self together so he will be ready for the ball when we send the invitations out.

My wish for you is twofold: 1) that you will have the faith, courage, and strength to withstand the Village Idiots, to defeat the Dragons, and never give up on creating your fairytale ending, and 2) in the words of Maya Angelou, that you "have enough courage to trust love one more time and always one more time."

If you have found your Happily Ever After and are interested in sharing your story with me, please contact me via my website, www.flippingthefairytale.com. I would love to hear from you. If you feel you need additional support in creating your fairytale, please go to my website and take the free assessment to unlock your dating persona and identify the areas that will drive you to success.

Afterword

Read on for an excerpt from Cindi Laree's forthcoming book, *Flipping the Fairytale – The Hopeless Romantic's Curse: Journey for the Cure.*

I think the curse of being a hopeless romantic is that if not treated properly it can become an addiction. And if we aren't careful, we can find ourselves looking for love in all the wrong places, or craving love and affection like a tweaker on day two in rehab. Only the difference between tweakers and hopeless romantics is that there is a program and a support system for tweakers, but hopeless romantics, well, the only thing offered to them is the Hallmark Channel for the good days, and the Lifetime Movie Network for the bad days.

No one truly understands what it is like to love so deeply, so easily, and then be crushed, devastated even, when it doesn't work out. Your friends tell you are supposed to "get over it" or "forget about it," like you didn't invest your time, your heart, and soul into this connection. Everyone has advice or criticism for your choices: "You should have known he was a Village

Idiot", or "That man had Dragon written all over him," or even, "How many more years are you going to stay in the wrong relationship with that Frog? Haven't you figured it out, he is never going to change!"

You are constantly chastised for looking at life through rose-colored glasses and not seeing that the world is dark and twisted. We are told that we don't understand how the real world works, because we want it to be full of fluffy bunnies, rainbows, and unicorns that poop jellybeans. They tell us that we are not in touch with reality, that we are lost in la-la-land.

Screw reality! There are cynics and haters on every corner, the news, social media, politics … everywhere we turn, there is hate and fear. And where hate and fear exist, they suck every ounce of love and light out of that space. And the hopeless romantics are left jonesing, looking for love, trying to find light and hope in the darkest of times. It is our curse. Nay, it is our misunderstood gift. Understanding this gift and how to share it with the world is, in fact, exactly the secret ingredient that makes a good casserole become great, a fine wine become divine, and a Lady-in-waiting become a Princess.

The world has enough cynics. Hate and fear are easy to share, because it takes no energy to perpetuate the dark. It is a default. Even when a light is introduced into the darkness, if nothing else happens with it, eventually, the light will fade. The bulb will burn out, the candle will melt, the flame will be extinguished, and darkness will prevail. The gift of the hopeless romantic is to see the beauty in all aspects of life, to see love in the most hopeless of situations. Even in the darkest of places, in the blackest of nights, a hopeless romantic can see even the slightest glimmer of light and bring love to this place. Their credo is as Maya Angelou has said: "Have enough courage to trust love one more time and always one more time." Ms. Angelou is a beautiful example of what a hopeless romantic should be, when they have transitioned from curse to cure, from a Lady-in-waiting to a Princess, and, in mastering the cure, transformed from a Princess into a Queen.

The cure is delivered to each of us in divine timing. For me, I received the cure during the time I was losing Johnny. It came as an answer to a prayer for help and guidance. At the time I wasn't sure that I could survive without him in my life. The answer was delivered to me in a dream, and it laid the framework for a new outlook on love. It provided healing to my wounded heart and gave me hope along with the power and courage to move forward.

Years have passed since I had this dream, I administered the cure, and leaned into my tweaker addiction to love. I have tasted the sweet sobriety and full embodiment of love, and I am ready to share this dream with you in hopes that I may quench your love addiction and move the hopeless romantic in each of us from curse to cure.

The Dream

I dreamed of a love so divine and so powerful that when I awoke, I realized it had transformed me from a Lady-in-waiting to a Princess in just one moment of awareness. I am not sure that you could even call it a dream, it felt so real.

In my dream, I was heartbroken and fearing the loss of a beautiful friendship. I sat alone in a small clearing in the woods, my face swollen and blotchy from tears. I was approached by a man, strong and statuesque. His size was intimidating, but his eyes were so kind that knew I had nothing to fear. He called out to me by name, and asked why I was so sad. I wondered if he was a Knight in Shining Armor, or a maybe someone's Prince, he was so perfect. He must belong to the Royal Guard or be a member of the High Council, I thought, as he seemed almost angel-like.

I told him of my struggles with finding love and happiness. I told him of my fear of never getting the chance to share the love I feel in my heart with someone who would reciprocate it. I told him of the connection I had felt to others, and how devastated I had been when it turned out they didn't feel the same for me. I cried as I told him of the heartbreak and loss I felt after each rejection or "friend zone" response. I loved all parts of love, but it seemed there was no one interested in receiving it from me.

The man patiently listened without interrupting. Then, as I looked at him through tear-filled eyes, he smiled at me softly and said, "Dear, sweet Princess. You have focused so much on giving your love to others, you have forgotten to share that love with yourself. You are caught up in a world where the true principles and intention of love have been manipulated, and love has been misrepresented as a destination, a utopia for those lucky enough to find it. Love, my sweet Princess, is not a destination. It is a journey."

I wasn't sure I understood what he was saying. All my life, I had wanted to be *in love*, in that utopia. Now he was telling me that it was an illusion? He asked if I would travel with him so that he could explain.

"Of course," I replied. I was desperately seeking the answers that would heal my heart.

He took my hand, and as if by magic, the forest opened up into a beautiful meadow. He said, "People view love as if it were a beautiful castle, a place where couples who have achieved the epitome of unconditional love arrive and are able to stay as long as they maintain their connection to one another. As romantic and relaxing as that may sound, the kind of love that makes you feel not just love but *loved* comes from action, and it must be built by each of us individually. It is not a place ready to move into, it is forged through trials, both successes and failures, and built from the ground up. Do you understand what I'm saying?"

"Kind of," I responded.

He smiled and said, "Watch this and let's see if it becomes clearer." I looked and saw the ground of the meadow begin to move. A firm foundation for a castle began to arise from the rocks, mud, and grass.

"The foundation of all love is radical self-love," he said. "Until you have built a solid foundation in radical self-love, any love that you give to others or love that others share with you will have no lasting foundation, and may crumble at any time."

Next, giant stone blocks began to appear. The castle walls were forming right before my eyes. He continued, "After self-love, next comes establishing unconditional love for all living things. This should be given freely to all, and is not something that needs to be earned. It is basic respect for mankind, the animals, and earth itself. This mutual love and respect given to all living things brings each of us the growth and opportunities to make our journey, find our life purpose, and share our light for others on their path. The walls of unconditional love provide shelter and protection from the chaos and storms of the outside world."

This was a new concept to me. I had always felt like loving someone unconditionally was like the icing on the cake, not the flour – a necessary ingredient to make the cake. I listened more intently as he continued.

"One of the issues that make this conceptually hard to grasp is that there are few people who understand the importance of unconditional love. Unconditional love and the shelter it creates for an individual to create and thrive are the load-bearing walls of society. If they are not set correctly, it is difficult to build a strong castle that will last the test of time. Do you understand, sweet Princess?"

I must have looked as confused as I felt. He smiled and went on.

"The cynics in society have perpetuated the myth that unconditional love is a reward only to be enjoyed by those who can weather the tests of time and patience. That it is a finite resource and must be given sparingly. When in fact, unconditional love, coupled with compassion and kindness, are infinite resources that will never diminish if they are shared and taught to others."

As he spoke, I could feel his words echoing through my soul. I could feel that he spoke truth. As I took this in, I watched as the area just outside the castle walls began to align, paths were created, and a large platform for gatherings emerged. I looked at him and asked, "Does love require a stage for karaoke?" He shook his head and with a glimmer in his eye responded "Absolutely! Every kingdom needs a place to sing power ballads, and love songs."

We both laughed. Then he smiled as he could see that my heart was beginning to heal. "Now the next step in the journey for love" he continued, "is in the creation of 'Common

Ground.' So if Self-Love is the foundation and Unconditional Love is the support, the next area for growth comes with common ground, commonality, and similar interests, like singing karaoke" He winked. "These common interests become the basis for strangers or villagers with whom you interact and develop respect and admiration for, or a sense of community with. People that you begin to recognize as on a similar journey, or who seem to have a similar energetic vibration. They may not be an exact match for you, but they are similar enough to you that you are comfortable with them and able to co-exist. There is a basic level of chemistry involved here."

As I understood it, he was saying that a common ground connection was primarily location-based – being at the same place at the same time – but with a limited degree of connectedness. Connections like this are out of sight, out of mind – like going to karaoke at the tavern. You are surrounded by people who also enjoy karaoke, you share some laughs, some refreshment, and some music, but then you go back to your life, family, career, etc., and you don't think about the people in the tavern until your next trip back to the tavern.

Meanwhile, on the grounds, benches and smaller gathering areas were being created.

We began to walk toward a newly erected bench as he said, "Each of the areas of new growth establish a higher level of connection, or an increased potential of love. The transition is from 'Common Ground' to 'Friendship.' It is similar to the commonality level, but the connections to these people become even clearer. It isn't just about the current circumstances that bring you together, it is about shared core beliefs, environments, bloodlines, or maybe even history together in your current lifetime."

I nodded. I was beginning to see how I had confused common ground with friendship, over and over again.

There was a noise from within the castle walls. "Come, Princess," he said. "Let me show you the next level."

We walked into the castle, and I saw that the interior walls were moving, creating different rooms. Tables, sinks, and furniture were being magically placed in their respective spots to create living spaces within the castle.

"The next level of love is that of the 'Family,' or, more specifically, familial love," he said. "This level strengthens the connections in Friendship and would include those relationships of family and others whom you adopt as your kin. You might call this 'A brother from another mother,' or 'A sister from another mister.' These would include parent and child, or best friends – strong bonds between people whose frequency continues to attract them to each other. This is Unconditional Love with a kick of, 'I know you are going to screw up, and possibly hurt me or anger me in this lifetime, but I will forgive you, because we are connected, and when you are hurting, part of me is hurting, too.'"

He continued to explain that at this level, those who are connected begin to contribute to the success of each other. You begin to feel connections with soul mates or relationships that seem to have connected in pre-existence or a previous lifetime. This connection is more: more love, more light, more risk of sharing your soul, but also more investment from all parties.

He then led me up a stone staircase to the master's quarters. We watched from the doorway as the furnishings were finding their places. I moved to step into the room, he stopped me by placing his hand on my shoulder and said, "This is the most sacred of the castle rooms and should only be shared with the most special of connections. This is reserved for 'Intimacy.' This is a level where the intimate bonds form. Where spiritual, emotional, and sometimes physical connections become strong, where it becomes safe to be who you truly are as a person, or at least safe to become who you are without judgment or competition."

As he spoke, I thought about my previous relationships – specifically with the Dragons, Village Idiots, and Frog Princes. It was clear that none of those archetypes deserved an opportunity to share a room like this with me. My mind snapped back to his words, and I knew I needed this guidance.

"This connection here is where contributing to their partners success becomes being committed to their success. Where the frequency that connects you to each other also connects you with Spirit. It is in this place that you challenge and inspire each other to attain your infinite potential. This is a place where anything is possible, and love has no expectation or rules – where respect is key. There is no fear, because at this high frequency, fear cannot exist. This is where soul mates and twin flames exist, if you believe in them. These are the soul contracts in which, together, you continue to seek joy, life purpose, and, through faith, a connection to the Divine. These are the people you have shared lifetimes or pre-existence with, and will spend eternity with on the other side. This is what is built with true intimacy."

He spoke of this connection with such reverence, such respect, it was no wonder that we were to only stand at the door and look in. The creation of this level of intimacy should be shared only with those who you love with all of your heart and soul.

"Is this the best it gets? Is this the last tier to build in the castle of love?" I asked, completely overwhelmed by the beauty and love that I had felt this day.

"Not quite, follow me."

He led me to a secret hall and up a winding staircase that seemed to go on forever. We must have been going into the highest spire of the castle. When the stairs ended and the room opened up, I saw a simple yet beautiful space, adorned with light blues, silver, and white. It looked as if we were walking into Heaven, or someplace not of this Kingdom. I was speechless.

"Here is where 'True Divinity' exists. This is the highest level of Love that ascends directly to the angels and Masters, the core of Source, and it is tied with the Divine. There is only God-like love here, it is the highest frequency. We are transcended into this realm through our compassion, empathy, kindness, unconditional love for our self and others, good works, forgiveness. Where you accept your Divine reward and become one with the Masters."

Tears rolled down my cheeks. The emotion that enveloped this room radiated the peace, joy, and love that I felt in every fiber of my being. I was in awe.

"It is time for me to go, Sweet Princess, but before I leave you please understand this: Your heart has been so lost trying to find the Love destination. That utopia does not exist, unless you create it. It must be created from the ground up, beginning with radical self-love and then unconditional love for all living things. Then you may grow and develop new relationships to experience other connections on the journey through love."

"Will my heart still get broken?" I asked.

"Yes, but the level at which we love someone, or we receive love from someone, is entirely up to each of us individually. There can be love between people from different places in their journey. Yes, it is real love, although it may not be the same level of love. It is possible to have a relationship between two people that exists in different realms. It is exactly this situation that you feel has broken your heart and brought you to tears in the woods where we met. Trust that your love is valuable, your loving heart is a gift. Your love is not rejected, it is simply not yet understood by the recipient – he is in a different place. Respect where he is, but never stop loving. When he is ready, his heart will open and he will receive higher levels of love."

I nodded tears freely flowing now. I was not ready for this beautiful man to leave, nor did I want to leave this place of Divine Love.

He squeezed my hand and said, "Do not be sad, for you now know the secrets and path to real love. It starts within you, and with loving others. Trust your heart and begin your journey. As you progress, opportunities for greater love will appear. You will establish common ground, forge friendships and familial bonds. You may find the intimate relationship that your heart desires, but through the journey of love you will reach a connection with true divinity, where you become a master of love, and create your fairytale ending. Go now, sweet Princess, and build your 'Happily Ever After.'"

In that moment, my eyes opened. I was returned to the couch in my living room, where I must have nodded off. I was disoriented, and my pillow was covered in tears. I could feel my heart beating in my chest. Tears continued to seep from my eyes, and I was acutely aware of the beautiful transformation that took place while I was sleeping. This journey would be the cure to my hopeless romantic curse, and I was ready to build my Kingdom of Love.

For more updates and new release information go to www.flippingthefairytale.com or email Cindi@CindiLaree.com.

Further Reading

Drawing Out the Dragons: A Meditation on Art, Destiny, and the Power of Choice, by James A. Owen

How to Get What You Really, Really, Really, Really Want, by Wayne Dyer and Deepak Chopra

Life's Golden Ticket, by Brendon Burchard

Mastery of Self, by Don Miguel Ruiz, Jr.

Mastery of Love and Relationships, by Don Miguel Ruiz

Acknowledgments

This book came about from my many failed attempts at finding romance and chasing my idea of what Happily Ever After looked like. I am truly grateful to all the men out there who made this book possible. Had you been my Prince Charming, I may not have found the passion and love I have in my life now.

Thank you to my girlfriends who were willing to share their stories with me and listen to my dating advice even though I was struggling myself: BreAnna, Kaitlan, and Rachel, thank you for trusting me as your guide.

Thank you to my Knights in Shining Armor, your insights into the male psyche were invaluable: Derek, Nick, Jeff, and Jim.

To Tommy, my Golden Knight, thank you for unlocking the magic in me. May you always know that life is good and the greatest love is unconditional.

To my Sisters and Fairy Godmothers:

Brittany, sister you have challenged me since the day you were born into my Kingdom, thank you for both saving my butt and being a pain in it. You are truly my soul mate, and I love you!

Becky, you have always been the nice one. Without your example and your willingness to help a sister out, whether it was listening to me cry about my frustrations and heartbreak or showing up to hang out for a weekend when I needed tears of laughter. In the words of Uncle Dave, Mooches Smooches!

Krissy, thank you for your support, and for being my go-to during my separation and divorce. I think I spent more time at your house than I did at my own. Thank you for being the castle walls while I fought my battle. I love and appreciate you!

To my Brothers, who I consider among the greatest Knights of the Roundtable, Curtis and Michael. Thank you for being good examples of what loving, supportive husbands should do. You have helped me in more ways than you will ever know! Love to you both!

To the King and Queen who brought me into this world, my parents. I love you Mom and Dad, I appreciate you more than you will even know.

To Dave, my ex-Prince Charming, thank you for your support; thank you for being an excellent co-parent. May you and your new Queen live Happily Ever After.

To my Tooth Fairy, Stacey! Thank you so much for your financial support to get me off and running. You were an answer to my prayers, and I will always remember you kindness and generosity.

To Patty, Jana, Bobbie, Kelly, Danielle, Stacey, and Kegan, the original fair maidens in my classes and in my tribe, thank you, ladies, for trusting me to provide you with insight and support. We have learned and grown together. Your faith in me and your encouragement have helped me follow my dreams and create my fairytale ending.

To the Author Incubator, Angela Lauria, and my book team, thank you for teaching me where the magic happens and helping me make this dream a reality.

To Maggie McReynolds, thank you for getting me ready for the ball! I couldn't have done it without your magic.

To the Morgan James Publishing team: Special thanks to David Hancock, CEO & Founder for believing in me and my message. To my Author Relations Manager, Niara Baskfield, thanks for making the process seamless and easy. Many more thanks to everyone else, but especially Jim Howard, Bethany Marshall, and Nickcole Watkins.

To the original Knight in Shining Armor, Tim, thank you for saving me from myself. Your guidance and support through the years has been gold. Thank you for being the friend who said what I needed to hear vs. what I wanted to hear, and never accepted my excuses. May you find the same love and happiness in your journey that I have found in mine. I love you, man!

Finally to my children, Kaitlyn, Ashley, and Nicholas, you are everything that is good in my Kingdom! Thank you for your unconditional love and support, not to mention your sense of humor to roll with my creation process. My wish for you is that you each love yourself as much as I love you. That radical self-love is what gives us the courage to go after our dreams, battle dragons, and save the world. Dream big, because dreams come true. Love more, because love is the antidote to fear. Create your fairytale ending, and know that you are all the biggest part of my Happily Ever After.

About the Author

Cindi Laree is a hopeless romantic turned intuitive life coach. She grew up in a small town in northern Arizona playing dress up with her friends as a child and singing along to Air Supply and New Kids on the Block in her teens. In college, she studied Theatre and Cinematic Arts, again dedicating her time and energy to make-believe. In 2012 Cindi's divorce was final after 13 years of marriage, at the time she so desperately wanted start over and to have a fairytale romance and live a passion filled Happily Ever After. Over the course of the last five years, she has developed and practiced "The Six Magic Keys to Unlocking Your Relationship Potential". In January of 2017 Cindi transitioned to intuitive life coaching on a full-time basis.

She has a gift for helping her clients unlock their sacred gifts and recognizing their passionate potential.

Cindi currently resides in Gilbert, AZ with her three children. When Cindi is not coaching, she enjoys playing coed softball and supporting her children in their various activities.

Website: www.flippingthefairytale.com

Email: Cindi@CindiLaree.com

Facebook: /Cindi.Bradley.Hostetler

Thank You

Hear Ye! Hear Ye!

A Royal Decree to All Fair Maidens throughout the Lands:

In sincere appreciation for your support, the Queen of Hearts wishes to bestow the following gifts and tokens upon you:

Free Membership in the Order of the Hearts: The royal newsletter and blog subscription to receive additional stories, insights, and healing messages from the Queen on her work.

Free Diagnostic Quiz: Use this quiz to determine the primary archetype that you attract in your life.

Free Strategy Session: Would you like to talk about your dating woes and identify some opportunities to release some of the fears and frustrations and create successful dating patterns? You can contact the Queen as well as get registered to receive any of these freebies by going to www.flippingthefairytale.com and registering under the "Freebies" section.

Morgan James
Speakers Group

www.TheMorganJamesSpeakersGroup.com

We connect Morgan James published
authors with live and online events
and audiences who will benefit
from their expertise.

Morgan James makes all of our titles available through the Library for All Charity Organization.

www.LibraryForAll.org

Printed in the USA
CPSIA information can be obtained
at www.ICGtesting.com
JSHW082355140824
68134JS00020B/2094

9 781683 507468

Hatches
and Seasons

10

Hatches

COLOR CODE

In general, flies that hatch in the spring and fall have dark-colored backs, and flies that hatch in the summer, beginning with PMDs in the West and Sulphurs in the East, are light colored.

WHAT THE TROUT SEE

When matching an insect, consider the belly color rather than the back color—the belly is what trout see (at least on the floating adults). Most insects are either a shade of olivish brown or light cream/yellow

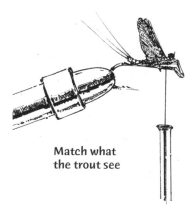

Match what the trout see

on their undersides, and if you carry imitations in these two major colors, in the right size and profile, you can match most mayflies.

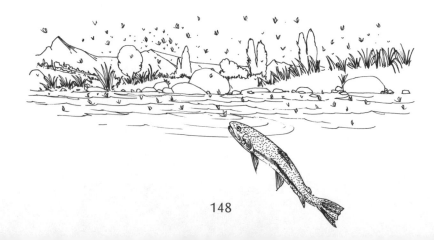

BACKLIGHTING

To detect spinners and other airborne bugs, look toward the sun. Insects are much easier to see when they are backlit.

USDA HARDINESS ZONE MAPS

Hardiness zone maps used for planting give you an idea of similar microhabitats. Catch a hatch later on streams in colder zones; earlier on streams in warmer zones. They are available for download from USDA (the National Arboretum) for state and country at http://www.usna .usda.gov/Hardzone/ushzmap.html. This one for the United States is from arborday.org/.

Look for Clues

Stonefly shucks on rocks indicate emerging stoneflies, swallows or other birds stitching the air may mean a hatch, inspect cobwebs for remnants of last night's hatch. Gasstation lights attract all sorts of bugs that hatch on rivers nearby.

2006 arborday.org Hardiness Zones Map

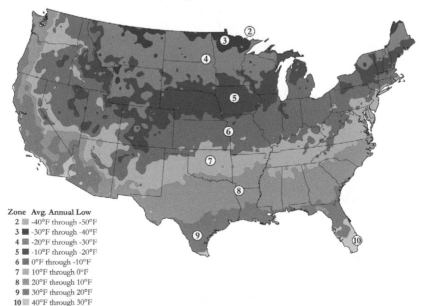

Zone Avg. Annual Low
2 ▦ -40°F through -50°F
3 ■ -30°F through -40°F
4 ▦ -20°F through -30°F
5 ■ -10°F through -20°F
6 ▦ 0°F through -10°F
7 ▦ 10°F through 0°F
8 ▦ 20°F through 10°F
9 ■ 30°F through 20°F
10 ▦ 40°F through 30°F

Mastering the Hatches

Charles Meck

The recipe for catching trout during a hatch is one part timing, one part preparation, and a healthy dose of luck.

Carry several sizes of the same pattern. Always carry the size that most appropriately matches the hatch, but also carry smaller patterns.

Carry several patterns that match the same hatch. For the most common hatches, I carry Catskill-style, parachute, and Compara-dun style versions of the same fly.

Sink the pattern, if changing size or pattern doesn't work.

Move during the hatch if you don't see risers. Don't be afraid to drive or walk up or downstream. Sometimes fish tend to pod up; other times, water or hatch conditions vary in a stream from one area to the next.

Clockwise from left: Catskill-style, parachute, and Compara-dun

Arrive at the right time. Know when the bugs hatch and be there. In the spring, fall, and winter this is often midday; in the summer, plan to be on the water late.

Fish on lousy days. Aquatic insects that hatch on overcast days tend to remain on the surface longer than when they hatch on bright sunny days. Trout are also less wary and feed more readily on cloudy, overcast days.

Fish tandem flies. Cover multiple bases with multiple flies. Fish both the adult and emerger, or emerger and nymph, or another combination. (For more on fishing two-fly rigs, read *Fishing Tandem Flies* [Headwater Books, 2007].)

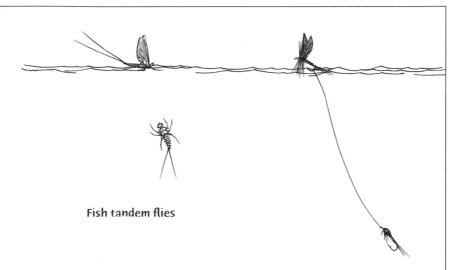

Fish tandem flies

Travel. Extend your fishing time for the super hatches—Green Drakes, for instance—by traveling from stream to stream, generally from south to north or from low to high elevation to follow the hatches at their peaks.

Location is everything. Sulphurs and drakes emerge in totally different areas of stream in different habitats. Drakes prefer silty bottoms; Sulphurs (and many other mayflies) prefer riffles. Learn and seek out the habitats different insects prefer.

Take time out to identify what is hatching. You don't need to know Latin, but sometimes a bug looks a different color or size up close than it does flying in the air. Take time to discern how fish are feeding on the insects: Are they boiling just under the surface or leaping out of the water? (See "Reading the Rise," page 154.)

Stonefly

Trico Time

John Barr

Tricorythodes *mayflies, Tricos for short, are one of the most widespread and predictable mayfly hatches in the country, occurring on many flowing waters from coast to coast. They can start hatching in late June and continue through October on a daily basis. Because they are so small and prolific, many fly fishers have trouble catching fish during a hatch.*

Trico duns usually hatch very early in the morning, sometimes in the dark. Unless you have some light on the water, the very small—generally size 20 and smaller—dun patterns can be difficult to see. Spinners are the most important stage to anglers because the spinner fall occurs later in the morning when the visibility is better, and trout love the easy meal of a dead spinner.

If trout are rising sporadically, they are probably feeding on the duns or some other insect. After the spinners hit the water's surface, the pace of the rising increases to a frenzied, rapid cadence. This is your tip that the trout are feeding on Trico spinners. Trout can get picky when feeding on Trico spinners, so you must have a good spinner pattern in the correct size.

The male Trico spinner is all black, and the female has a black thorax and pale-olive abdomen. I have heard of places where trout key on the two-toned females, but all-black patterns have always worked fine for me.

When the Tricos start hatching early in the season, they can be as large as a size 18. As the months progress, they get smaller and can be a size 26 or smaller in October. The density of the hatch and spinner fall also decreases as the months progress. Carry a good selection of sizes in your Trico box.

A dead drift is essential to success. Trico spinners are dead and motionless, and trout will not take a waking spinner. For years I fished a single floating spinner pattern. The small, flush-floating fly was difficult to see, and it was hard to tell if I was getting a drag-free drift.

Fish a Trico spinner fall with a floating, black-bodied Trico Vis-A-Dun, with a sunken spinner tied off the bend on 6 inches of 6X tippet. The Vis-A-Dun lets me know I am getting a drag-free drift, and with the grizzly hackle clipped on the bottom, it is regularly taken as a spinner. If a trout takes the drowned spinner, the Vis-A-Dun acts as a strike indicator.

Natural spinners may cover the surface and compete with a floating pattern. A drowned spinner stands out better.

When trout quit feeding on surface spinners, they often move to the heads of runs and feed on drowned spinners. In this situation, I fish a size 10 hopper, a size 18 black Copper John, and a drowned spinner combination and can usually count on an hour or two of good fishing.

I use 6X premium-grade fluorocarbon tippet when fishing spinners.

Trico clouds

BEAT THE BRUSH

To match the hatch, get a sample. Many types of hatching insects fly and rest in streamside vegetation. It's easier to ambush them there than capture them on the wing.

WATCH THE BIRDS

Birds such as waxwings and swallows (and a host of others) get active when bugs hatch. Even when you can't see them, bugs may be present if you see the birds dipping and darting in the air.

PRESENTATION IS KEY

Most of the time, on most of the streams throughout the United States, nothing is hatching. Trout have to be opportunistic feeders, and if your presentation is good and pattern imitates something a trout eats, you are ahead of the game.

READING THE RISE

Trout behave differently on different rivers, and though anglers over the years have tried to describe the nature of riseforms, we can do so only generally. Here are tips to help you figure out what the fish are feeding on. Use these clues along with other indicators, such as time of year, time of day, and visible insects.

Use a pair of binoculars to determine riseforms from afar.

When trout are feeding on small flies, their riseforms are usually small with few splashes.

Splashier rises tend to come from immature trout or fish chasing

Beat the brush

caddis or other fast-moving insects like damselflies and stoneflies.

Bulges or boils below the surface mean fish are feeding on emergers and indicate that an emerger, soft-hackle, or other wet is the best choice. Pay careful attention to rises to determine whether the riseform is from a fish feeding on or slightly below the surface.

Porpoising trout often show head, back, fins, and tail and tend to feed on emerging mayflies or midge pupae, and sometimes surface insects (look for bubbles). Some-times you just see the back and not the head.

Sipping trout are feeding on small flies—mayfly emergers, spin-ners, small terrestrials such as bee-

Bulging rise

Porpoising trout

Porpoising trout (headless)

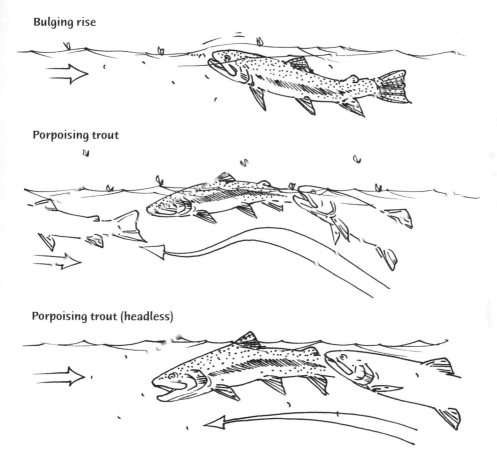

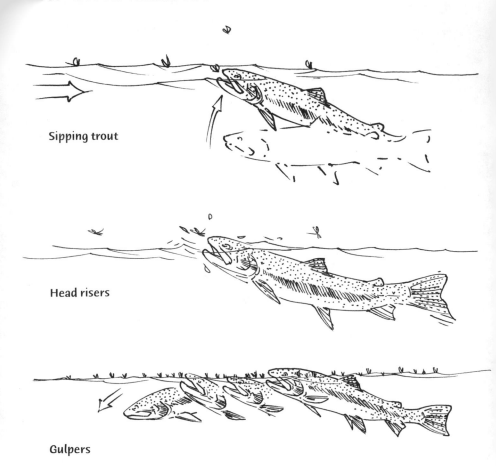

Sipping trout

Head risers

Gulpers

tles and ants—in the surface film or on the surface. These riseforms may also indicate fish are taking spinners in the surface film. On smooth water, the trout may leave a few small bubbles, but these rises are hard to detect in broken currents.

Head risers are feeding on insects at the surface and their heads come entirely out of the water. Unlike sipping risers, you can usually determine the size of a head riser by the size of the head and their wake. They leave behind telltale bubbles when returning to the water.

Gulpers are a breed of head risers, working on a faster rhythm, usually feeding on profuse hatches

Flying trout

Tailing trout

of insects on flat water, such as Trico spinner falls or *Callibaetis.* In slow-moving or still water, mark the direction gulpers are moving and place your fly in their path. Don't cast where they last rose.

Fish leaping out of the water are what Montana guide E. Neale Streeks calls "flying trout." Depend-ing on time of year and time of day, this usually signifies fish taking cad-dis emergers or damselflies or drag-onflies (midday in the summer).

Tailing trout. When trout root headfirst for cressbugs or scuds in bottom vegetation they often wave their tails in or slightly above the water like redfish.

Fishing Pods

George Anderson

Pods, large groups of feeding fish, provide exciting and demanding fishing.

Approach from below the pod. Accuracy is key, so get as close as you can. I often get within 15 to 20 feet of my target—close enough to observe the individual rises and feeding patterns of the fish.

Have a plan. If you cast into the pod, all the fish will spook and scatter. Strategize about how to catch as many fish as possible. That may mean picking off fish at the tail of the pod or fish feeding off to the side. If you are not after numbers, stalk the largest trout.

Pick steady risers. Don't waste your time on sporadic risers, unless they are large.

Many trout rise at regular intervals. Predict when the trout will rise and time your casts accordingly.

Focus on individuals. Don't cast into the group and hope that one eats your fly.

Don't waste too much time on one fish. If I can't get a trout to take after a half-dozen good casts, I pick another target.

If you have tricky surface currents, change your casting position slightly or put more slack in the leader and tippet by mending or using a slack-line, pile, or curve cast.

For utmost accuracy, I drive the line directly over the rod tip on the forward cast so that the leader and tippet lay out straight toward the fish, rather than hooking or slicing in at an odd angle.

Most anglers cast too far upstream of the fish. The fly should land between 8 and 15 inches ahead of the fish and on a path that will take it directly over its nose.

Seeing small flies can be difficult, but if you cast a straight line, you should know approximately where your fly is on the surface. If you see a fish rise within a foot or two of that spot, set the hook.

Sometimes I fire the fly at the surface a little harder than normal to make it easier for me to see where the fly hits the water. Slamming down a spinner can make it sink a little, and submerged spinners are very effective.

When you hook a fish, the best scenario is that it peels away from the pod. If it runs into the pod, I immediately slack off pressure to calm it and prevent it from cartwheeling through the pool. When the fish heads back downstream, I apply the heat and move it away from the pod.

Sometimes you can't help but put down the pod after hooking a fish. Be patient. After 10 minutes or so, the pod usually starts feeding again.

A pecking order in most pods puts the largest fish up front. Going for Mr. Big by casting over his buddies won't work. Get above the pod and drift your fly downstream with a combination of a reach cast and mending. Your first casts are critical.

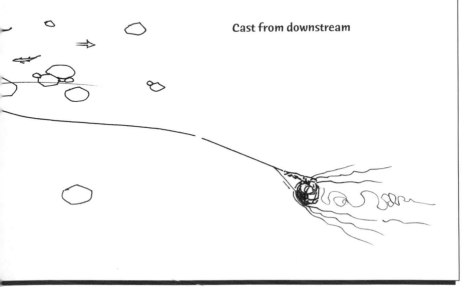

Cast from downstream

Tips for Catching Selective, Rising Trout

Mike Lawson

Many consider casting to selective trout rising to hatching insects the essence of fly fishing, but it can be frustratingly difficult.

Time spent studying a trout's feeding rhythm is often more productive than repeatedly casting over the same trout. Your best chance is your first cast.

If you don't know what fly to use, study the water with binoculars or use a small insect net to seine the water close by. Select a fly that is the approximate size and color of the natural.

Get Close

Getting close reduces the need to false-cast, and the closer you are, the more accurate your casts.

Although you may know what insect a trout is eating, you must determine whether it is feeding on, in, or just under the surface film. You can determine if the fish is feeding on or in the surface by watching individual insects with binoculars as they drift over the feeding fish.

When you approach a rising trout, wade as quietly and carefully as possible so you don't make too much disturbance in the water and to minimize the sound of your wading boots grinding against the bottom.

After you get into position, wait for the trout to rise a couple of times before you make your first cast.

If you put a trout down and it stops feeding, stay in position and wait 5 minutes or so. It will often start feeding again. Don't forget to look around. Sometimes a spooked fish will change locations and start rising again.

Draw the trout's attention to your fly--if the surface is covered with aquatic insects—by giving it a subtle twitch just as it starts to enter the trout's window of vision.

When you need to use a small fly or emerger to match the hatch, you can attach the small hatch-matching pattern as a dropper 8 to 12 inches from a larger fly.

Unmatch the Hatch

If the surface is covered with aquatic insects, sometimes you need to use something different like a Royal Wulff, Parachute Adams, or beetle to draw the trout's attention. It should be about the same size as the naturals.

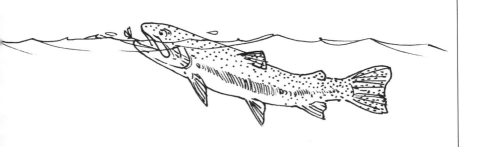

11

Seasons

SPRING
The Phenological Fly

Mayfly hatches coincide with bloom periods of common trees and flowers. Learn to recognize these patterns and record them in a journal.

Hatch-matcher Charles Meck first planted the seed of this idea in *Great Rivers, Great Hatches*. Canadian Bob Scammell contributed to the body of knowledge of Western hatches with *The Phenological Fly*.

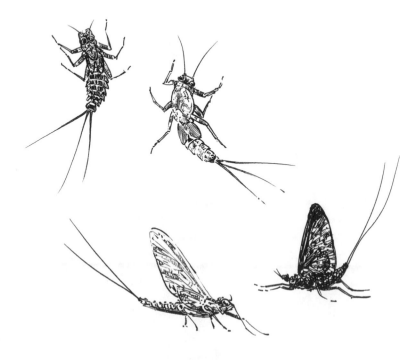

For example, in Pennsylvania, blooming forsythia or wild ginger indicate that anglers should be on the lookout for Hendricksons, blooming mountain laurel signifies Slate Drake time, and wild rhododendron, Tricos. According to Scammell, sighting brown-eyed Susans mean *Hexagenia* are emerging, and at the first signs of clematis blooms, he starts looking for Western March Brown in his neck of the woods, Alberta.

When watching plants and flowers, wild specimens are best because microhabitats near houses and in suburban gardens can expedite bloom times.

Hunter-Gatherer

Even catch-and-release anglers can show their spouses that time spent wandering in the woods is not in vain. In the spring, hunt for morels and gather fiddleheads, which are delicacies at the table.

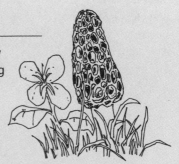

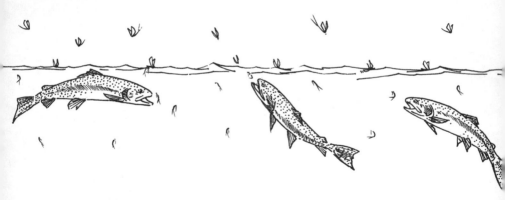

Splat Tactics

When casting inchworms, beetles, hoppers, and other terrestrials, don't be bashful about splatting the fly on the surface of the water. The naturals often fall into the water less than gracefully, and the disturbance attracts fish.

Runoff

Spring means runoff, but different streams will be in different stages. Learn what streams drop and clear quicker than others to maximize your fishing time. These streams may also clear faster after a summer rainstorm.

Fish When It's Warmest

In the spring, most mayflies hatch in the midafternoon into evening.

Go Deep in Colder Water

In general, higher, colder water means less surface activity. Fish streamers and nymphs more frequently in the spring or hang a nymph dropper off of your dry fly.

Fish Eggs

Suckers and rainbow trout spawn in the spring, so egg patterns can be effective.

Henry's
Fork Hopper

SUMMER
Trico Time
Summer's main game is Tricos in the morning, but you can fish terrestrials midday and find rising fish near dark. For the brave of heart, night fishing (see page 47) offers shots at big browns.

Terrestrial Tactics
Size down your hoppers.
Fly shops sell a lot of large hopper patterns, but naturals come in all sizes and smaller patterns may surprise fish.

On many streams, crickets are a wise alternative to hoppers. Anglers don't fish cricket patterns as much as hoppers, yet they are as abundant, even more so in wooded areas.

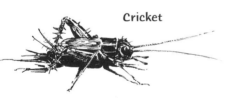

Cricket

Sink any terrestrial with split shot or tie some weighted ones ahead of time. Trout are suckers for sunken hoppers, inchworms, and ants.

Stealth Flies
Low water makes it easier to find fish and to wade about, but also makes fish warier. Trade heavy-hackled spring patterns for flush-floating ones.

Anticipate Ants
Flying ants migrate in late summer and fall, and often fall into the water, causing periods of feeding frenzy. These migrations are often predictable, so ask around. Carry simple Antron- or CDC-winged patterns in your box.

Fish Faster Water
Look for fish in faster, more oxygenated water. Wet wade to find the spring holes where fish congregate in warmer water temperatures. Note these spots for your winter fishing as well.

Seek the Shade
Seek out and fish in the shade—whether entire pools, or shaded spots in a particular pool. Don't spend too much time on water baking in the sun. Bridges are always a good bet.

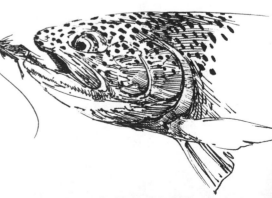

Sun and Mosquitoes

Baseball caps are popular fly-fishing headgear, but they do a poor job of protecting your head and neck from the sun. Carry a bandana and tuck it under the back of your cap if you are out in the sun; wet it for cool relief on a hot day.

Long-sleeve shirts are warmer than short-sleeve shirts, but they protect your arms from sun and bugs a lot better.

Wear lightweight Capilene or polypro long underwear under your breathable waders in the summer to help transfer sweat and keep you from feeling clammy. Plus, they add a layer of warmth if you are wading in colder tailwaters. Air temps may be hot, but the water may not.

Apply sunscreen before you go fishing, and wash your hands. When you reapply it regularly through the day, apply it with the back of your hand so that you don't get it on your fly line. Put on your bug dope before fishing as well—after you apply the sunscreen. Most experts agree that you should buy individual and not combination products.

Carry lip balm with you and use it regularly to protect your lips from burning.

Drink lots of water through the day—at least two quarts. If you're taking a long trip but can't carry a lot of water, drink lots on the car ride to your fishing spot.

Do not put sunblock on your forehead—it can drip into your eyes (wear a hat to protect that part of your face). Even if the bottle says its tearproof, sweatproof, waterproof, it probably is not. Baby sunblocks are most likely to be tear-free. Use SPF 30 or higher.

Many saltwater flats guides wear thin balaclavas over their faces and gloves on their hands, trading the mild discomfort of additional clothing for the enhanced protection against the sun.

Don't get DEET on your fly line

Lightning Tips

According to the National Oceanic and Atmospheric Administration (NOAA) National Weather Service, approximately 1,800 thunderstorms are occurring at any given time, about 16 million thunderstorms each year. Most thunderstorms last about 30 minutes and are typically about 15 miles (24 km) in diameter.

Count the seconds (one thousand one, one thousand two) between seeing the lightning and hearing the first sound of thunder and divide by 5 to get the approximate distance of the storm in miles. Sound in the atmosphere travels just under a mile in 5 seconds.

Sharply defined streaks of lightning are probably close. If you see a flash but not bolts, the storm is likely farther away. Sharp, abrupt thunderclaps are very close; rumbles farther away.

To determine storm size, follow the steps for determining the distance, but continue counting as long as you can hear the faint rumblings of thunder. Subtract this number from the number you got when calculating the distance of the storm based on the first sound of thunder for the storm's approximate size.

Avoid water, high ground, open spaces, all metal objects including fences, machinery, motors, and large natural objects such as trees and boulders that can attract lightning.

Seek safety in a large building (preferably one with steel girders) or a car (with windows completely shut). The metal frame conducts electrical charge and passes it along to the ground. If lightning strikes a tree, the charge can transmit through the ground through the roots, so don't seek safety under a tree. Some experts say that if the tree is your only option, then pick one with a deep root system, such as an oak tree.

If lightning strikes nearby when you are outside, crouch down, place your hands over your ears to minimize hearing damage from thunder, and stay at least 15 feet away from other people.

If out in a boat, stay in the center of the cabin if you can. If there is no cabin, stay low in the boat. Keep arms and legs in the boat and out of the water. Stop fishing and put down your rods and anything else you might have in your hands. Do not talk on your cell phone. Disconnect electronic equipment and lower antennae.

FALL

Water in the fall is typically low and clear, and fish have had a season's education about the latest fly patterns. You must have excellent presentations and approach.

Most fish species feed heavily to prepare for winter and streams are less crowded, making fall an ideal time to be on the water.

Brown and brook trout spawn in the fall, so you may catch aggressive and territorial males if you fish streamers.

Steelhead ascend rivers with fall rains

Stand Out

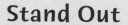

Wear at least one article of fluorescent-orange clothing when fishing during hunting season. Fall is not the time to blend in with your environment.

Bring a fleece jacket or a parka even if the weather forecast is nice. Fall weather can change quickly.

Fish feed earlier in the day, like in spring.

Flies are dark in the fall and dry fly selections relatively simple: out West, *Baetis,* October Caddis, and Tricos can be important; in the East, *Baetis,* Tricos, and *Isonychia* are important.

Sculpin

WINTER

Flat-Water Risers

If you are looking for risers on a nice winter day, concentrate on flat water in pools as well as shallow water that warms quickly.

Small Flies

Cold-weather bugs are almost always small and mostly midges. In late winter and early spring, *Baetis* and black stoneflies can hatch, but they are also small. Fill your winter box with mostly small subsurface patterns, a few dry flies for those opportunities when they arise, and a few meat-and-potatoes flies such as stonefly nymphs and streamers. Egg patterns are also excellent choices.

Slow and Low

The colder the water, the deeper and slower you should fish your fly. Fish won't move far to take streamers, so try dead-drifting them under an indicator. Break the water into rows and methodically fish each one.

Spring Creeks and Tailwaters

Focus on springs creeks and tailwaters, which don't freeze in the winter and have more stable water temperatures.

Don't Leave Fish to Find Fish

Winter fish tend to pod up, so if you catch one, don't move to a better spot. You're probably in it.

Ice-Free Guides

Chapstick, Vaseline, or cooking spray on your guides reduces the amount of ice build-up.

Fish Smarter

Once the guides ice up, use roll and Spey casts to fish as much as possible without stripping in line. With these casts, you can also keep your hands toasty in mittens.

Think Spring

Springs entering a river keep water cool in the summer and ice free in the winter.

Staying Warm

The key to staying safe in the winter (and enjoying yourself).

Don't go into the water if you don't have to.

Bring a spare set of clothes and keep them in your vehicle for emergencies. Carry a waterproof case of strike-anywhere matches in case you need to build a fire.

Boot-foot waders are warmer than stocking foots because they are generally less constricting and allow more circulation. Regardless of boot type, make sure there's room in your boots and your feet aren't constricted. Wool and most other materials provide insulation by trapping warm air in the spaces and in the fibers. If your wading boots are too tight, even good socks can't perform their function.

Breathable waders are fine in winter—if you layer properly. Start with a thin, tight base layer that wicks moisture and keeps your skin dry and then add one or two layers of fleece pants—depending on the air and water temperature. Your waders should keep your lower body warm under all but the most severe conditions. Wear thin sock liners and good socks.

A warm fleece or wool hat under the hood of your wading jacket can keep you warm on cold days. An exposed head loses body heat quickly. If you get warm in the afternoon, your hat may be the only layer you need to remove.

Fish a fixed length of line by roll casting

Warm packs designed for boots and gloves provide a quick source of heat (Grabber Mycoal is one popular brand).

Bring two or three pairs of wool, fleece, or neoprene fingerless gloves on cold winter days. Leave an extra pair of mittens in the car just in case. An extra pair of dry gloves in your vest can keep you fishing after everyone else goes home. Stuff some inexpensive liner gloves into your vest or pack. They don't take up space, but you'll appreciate the spare set if you get your main gloves wet or leave them at home.

Bloodflow to your feet and hands decreases when your core body temperature decreases. Keep your extremities warm by properly layering your torso and legs to keep your core body temperature warm.

Sole Savvy

Felt soles collect snow and become cumbersome and dangerous. Sticky rubber soles—such as the Aquastealth brand—with studs are best.

Eat lots of protein, carbohydrates, and fats. You need to keep the fires stoked to stay warm. Bring along a thermos of your favorite hot beverage. Prime it by pouring boiling water into it and letting that sit for 10 minutes or so before dumping it out and putting in your drink.

Save the alcohol until you're inside. We feel cold when blood flows from our skin into the organs to keep our core temperature warm. After drinking alcohol, blood flows to the skin (making us feel warm and our faces flush), which makes our core body temperature decrease rapidly.

Frosty Freestoners

Joe Cambridge

Anglers usually head for spring creeks or tailwaters in the winter, if they head out at all. But freestone streams can also provide some good winter fishing.

Mid morning to early afternoon is the magic window—when it's the warmest—so sleep late and be off the water long before supper.

Carry a variety of nymphs and midge pupa imitations—most of the action will be subsurface.

Ruffed grouse can sometimes provide clues to the whereabouts of winter trout. Seeking protection from the elements, the birds often pick spots where heavy pine cover reduces wind chill and spring water seeps from the ground. Note the places where you flush grouse regularly, and carefully work any holes or holding areas just downstream of these areas.

Walk or cross-country ski on days when fishing is impossible to note any open water, which are likely locations of springs. Binoculars help you search terrain without trudging through snow.

Find the Fish

Look for spots where water temperatures are highest and current speeds are more suited to a trout's slow metabolism at this time of year. Bridge holes where steady sun warms the concrete and nearby water are good bets.

Don't fish your favorite bamboo or most expensive graphite stick. Use a rod you won't miss if the worst happens. Falls are not uncommon in snow and ice. Should you slip, you're likely to go to your strong hand to catch yourself, so learn to carry your rod in the weak hand and keep the tip pointed behind you.

Avoid standing in one place for too long in cold water. When you decide to move, your legs won't work well, and next comes the unpleasant, dangerous bath. Force yourself to get out and move around once in a while to keep the circulation going.

Avoid crunching or collapsing the thin layer of ice lining the shore on your approach. Such noise carries a long way and alerts trout to your presence.

Timing Is Everything

Fish during the warmest part of the day; fish in the warmest water.

If the sun is out, stay back from the bank, especially if you're seeing "soot flies," the little stoneflies that look like wood ashes come alive. Even a pale-winter sun can get them hatching. Never splash through the shallows of a deep hole. Large trout sometimes hold in the sun-warmed shallows in water barely deep enough to cover their dorsals. They're not just there to keep warm; they are hunting the small, dark stoneflies scuttling out of the creek.

Carry binoculars so you can look for feeding trout without having to trudge through the snow. Even better, you may be able to scan the water from the comfort of your vehicle.

PART 4

Travel, Destinations, and Species Other Than Trout

12

Travel, Destinations, and Species Other Than Trout

GENERAL TRAVEL TRIPS

Use a checklist. Print one out, or save different ones for each fishing trip, especially if boating or camping. Create your own list on a computer and revise as necessary. Depending on your needs, you might prepare one for overseas travel, boat trips, saltwater trips, and so on.

Even on short trips, always put a spare rod in the car in case you break your main one.

Hide your keys near the car rather than carrying them with you to the

176

river. Tell your fishing buddy where they are in case of an emergency.

Don't plan on cell-phone coverage. Always tell someone where you are going or leave a note.

Purchase trip insurance that includes medical and medical evacuation insurance when traveling out of the country.

Rent a satellite phone for trips out of the country and hope you never have to use it. They are affordable insurance where cell phones don't work.

Buy licenses ahead of time online or over the phone through each state's fish and game department.

Keep your license in the same place, with equipment you always take fishing.

Tape inventory lists to your gear-storage boxes (Rubbermaid containers work well). That way you know what you have and what you need to replace in each box (this also works well for camping and cooking gear).

If possible, ship important gear to your destination ahead of time. That way, by the time you leave, you know your gear is waiting there for you, safe and sound.

DO YOUR HOMEWORK

Before you take a trip, whether it is to a new lodge 1,000 miles away or a closer jaunt, it pays to do a little research.

New School

Fly-fishing websites such as flyfisherman.com or danblanton.com have a treasure trove of information on them, so they are often a good place to begin searching for information. Before posting a question on the bulletin boards, remember to search through the archive of posts if the website has one. You don't want to ask a question that has already been answered, if you can help it.

Other recreational sites also provide information about fishing or water conditions. Many die-hard fly fishers monitor gear-fishing websites for fishing news. Surfing sites, for instance, provide information on

Online Mapping

Websites are great for trip planning. You can view satellite maps of a stream on many different websites such as Google Earth (earth.google.com) or terraserver.com.

ocean water conditions. Canoe or kayak websites often provide good information about boat launches or popular floats.

USGS streamflow data (water-data.usgs.gov/nwis) provides the best online resource for water conditions. Only familiarity with local water conditions will help you decipher the flow's impact on water clarity and other conditions, but in time and with practice, you'll be able to check streamflow to gauge the fishing conditions.

Bookmark your favorite weather website such as weather.com, and be sure to check it frequently before a trip. Compare past to predicted weather to identify trends that can affect fishing.

Old School

Purchase a *Delorme Atlas and Gazetter* for your state and other states that you fish frequently, and keep it in the car. Write notes on the map or on sticky notes.

Don't forget how helpful libraries can be. You can order magazine article reprints from Interlibrary Loan (if your library doesn't carry the magazine), which is often easier (and cheaper) than trying to find a back issue another way.

Being able to read a topographic map is an invaluable skill for fly fishers. With a basic understanding, you can look at a topo map of an area and reliably predict the character of the stream—as well as the nature of access. The narrower the

lines, the steeper the ascent. Contour lines form V shapes in valleys or along stream beds. The point of the V points uphill.

Verify any information you glean from books, articles, fly-shop owners, and online bulletin boards with another source. Buy several guidebooks and compare them; call a fly shop after reading a report online. There is some flat-out bad information out there; but more often, people just have different experiences and opinions, so it helps to gather as much info as you can before embarking on your trip. Have realistic expectations. Some people really exaggerate fishing conditions and fish size.

Solicit local advice, but use your own common sense.

BEAR AWARE

Drowning presents a greater threat to fly fishers, but fishing several of the world's best fly-fishing destination involve sharing the water with bears. Here are some tips to prevent unpleasant encounters.

Carry bear spray in an accessible spot such as on your wading belt or pack shoulder strap, especially if you are fishing in grizzly country. Arrange to purchase it at your destination if you are flying because airlines don't allow it, even if it is packed in baggage.

Practice with the bear spray at least once by discharging some of it. This will give you some indication of how far and wide the spray travels. Follow manufacturer's instructions.

GUIDES

Even for experts, good guides are worth the expense because they can show you how to fish unfamiliar water, they often have a boat, they often have access to private water or know of less crowded areas, and they can arrange transportation and gear if you are traveling on business and want to get in a day of fishing. But you have a right to make sure you get what you pay for.

Unless you ask them to, good guides don't fish while they are working.

The best guides are good teachers. Tell them what you'd like to learn, and listen to what they have to tell you.

Be honest about your abilities right up front with the guide. They'll find out soon enough and honesty will save some embarrassing moments.

Have realistic expectations. Be fair to yourself and your guide. Your guide should work hard for you, but some days just weren't meant to be.

If you have special dietary requirements, tell the guide well in advance, not just before the drift-boat launches.

Before you book the trip, ask about tips, meals, transportation to and from the launch, how long you fish each day, who provides flies, etc.

Avoid surprising a bear. Make noise, especially where the sound of the flowing water can muffle your approach. Walk and camp in larger groups when in bear country. Wear a bear bell or sing while you walk, especially around blind corners.

When bears are also fishing nearby, such as on many Alaska streams, always give them plenty of room. If a bear approaches you, stop fishing and move away. Give a splashing fish slack, or cut the line, if the bear is interested in it.

Keep a clean camp. That means nothing but ashes in your fire pit, no food or water in your tent, hang a bear bag at least 50 yards from

Some guides provide lunch and drinks; others do not. In Florida, for instance, it is customary for you to provide your guide's drinks and lunch.

Don't let the number of fish you catch solely determine the size of your tip.

On group trips you may have to rotate guides. Some anglers like this and others do not. While it takes a while to learn how to communicate with your guide, some anglers don't want to get stuck with the same guide (especially one they don't mesh with) for the entire time. Understand how the guide/client rotation works *before* you go to a lodge or on a group trip. Also, keep an open mind: just because you don't have the lodge's best guide for the day doesn't mean you won't have good fishing and/or get along well with the guide that you do have.

The best guides are good teachers

your camp, don't clean fish near camp, stand upwind when cooking food to prevent your clothes from smelling like food, and other commonsense practices to avoid enticing trouble. Bears like food and are attracted by the smell, so don't encourage them.

Steer Clear Of

Bear cubs. Mothers may be nearby.

Dead animals such as elk, deer, cattle, etc. Grizzlies are protective of their food and may be nearby.

Feeding grounds such as berry fields (black and grizzly) or stands of whitebark pine trees (grizzly).

Backcountry Fishing

Ross Purnell

Put some distance between you and the crowds for the best fishing.

Preventing Dehydration

Drink at least 64 ounces of water per day when you are hiking or fishing. In hot weather or long hikes, you will use twice that much. Water is heavy, and filter systems are slow when you are thirsty. Use water-treatment drops (Aquamira or similar) to kill bacteria in water that is otherwise clear and drinkable. It's a tasteless treatment that saves weight and allows you to drink as much as you want. (Iodine tablets leave a bad taste in the water.)

Don't carry your multipiece rod in an aluminum tube. It adds weight, bulk, and makes it hard to attach to the outside of your pack. Carry your 3-, 4-, or 5-piece rod in the sock, strapped to the side of your pack. As long as the rod is secured properly, and the pack is longer than the unassembled rod pieces, the bulk of the pack will protect the rod.

Always hike with a buddy in the backcountry. Let someone know where you'll be hiking and fishing and when you are expected to return. Cell phones have limited coverage in remote areas so don't expect them to work.

Bring a hand-held GPS device along with your standard maps so you always know your position. You can determine the coordinates of your fishing destination beforehand using Google Earth, TravelByGPS.com, or a similar online application.

Leave the waders at home and plan on wet wading if you plan on hiking long distances in the warm summer months. Waders are too bulky and heavy to be worth the effort for a day trip, and are also impractical for overnight trips when you also must pack a tent, sleeping bag, and food.

Never wear cotton outdoors

Once it is wet, it stays wet—wet cotton is heavy and cold and a recipe for hypothermia. Avoid cotton (even cotton underwear) especially when wet wading, when hiking long distances to fish, or when you'll be camping in the backcountry. Your wet cotton clothing will not be dry in the morning.

Wear two pairs of socks for hiking and wet wading. Liner socks should be made from a thin, tight, synthetic material that wicks moisture out. This buffer layer protects your skin from blisters. Women's ankle-high pantyhose socks are a cheap alternative to brand-name liner socks.

Wear a thick, cushioning outer sock like heavyweight Capilene or SmartWool to help protect your feet at friction points including the back of your heel or the outside of your big toe. A two-sock system protects against blisters even when your shoes are soaked from wading.

Hiking in felt-soled wading boots is dangerous and will quickly wear out your soles. You'll be hiking more than wading, so wear lightweight hikers with stiff soles and aggressive treads.

continued on page 184

Backcountry Fishing continued

Layering is lightweight and more comfortable through a greater temperature range. Instead of a single heavy warm jacket, wear a tight synthetic base layer (cool when worn alone, dry and warm when layered). Bring a fleece and a water- and windproof jacket for an outer layer.

To ensure a warm sleep in a lightweight sleeping bag, use a closed-cell foam mattress or self-inflating mattress, and bring a lightweight polypropylene hat for sleeping. These two items are lighter and will keep you more comfortable than a bulky four-season sleeping bag.

Keep your fishing stuff—fly boxes, sunglasses, reel—in your pack's outside pockets. It's not uncommon to stop along the way on many hiking/fishing trips, and it can be frustrating if your fishing gear is at the bottom of your pack.

Simplify

Create a single fly box with flies suited for mountain streams and high lakes. Parachute Adams (#10–20), CDC & Elks (#14–16), foam beetles (#12–14), and foam ants (#16–20) are all you need in most alpine areas.

Aluminum-tipped trekking poles take some strain off your ankles and knees on rugged hikes and also make good wading staves.

Many national parks and other wilderness preserves do not allow fires. Stoves—along with the associated cookware—are cumbersome. On short one- or two-night trips, eat ready-to-eat, high-energy foods like beef jerky, energy bars, granola bars, and trail mix, nuts, and candy. This saves time so you can fish more, and saves space so you can pack extra fishing gear. Drink plenty of water with dehydrated foods like jerky and dried fruit.

Saltwater Travel Tips

Lefty Kreh

Many saltwater trips involve travel far afield and new tackle for lots of trout fishers.

Contact the locals. Before you make firm plans, call the guide, outfitter, or lodge you are fishing with and get updates on conditions.

Do your research. Ask guides and lodges for a list of references and call their references. Good guides should have a long list, not just a few names. Ask others who have fished the location who the best guides are, and try to get those guides. Request top guides in advance. Read as much as you can about your destination online, in magazines, or books.

Travel during the best times. Many fly-fishing destinations have peak periods of prime fishing. Plan to go at those times.

Know the tides. Tide has everything to do with the habits of fish. Research tides in advance, so you can plan for the best fishing.

When in a boat, always put on your raingear before motoring out. I prefer bib-type pants; regular rain pants can slip down when you sit, exposing your bottom and waist to rain and sea spray.

Copy your passport. Make several copies of the first page of your passport and store them separate from the original. If your passport is stolen or lost, you will have the information you need to get a replacement.

A waterproof bag for your valuables and items that can't get wet (cell phone, wallet, snack, digital camera) is invaluable if you will be spending any time in a boat, especially a moving boat when water splashes up and over the bow. Put the bag in a boat's dry storage for extra protection.

Consider other species. Be prepared to fish for species other than the ones you set out to catch because conditions are not always favorable. On a billfish trip I took, for example, the billfish were not around, so I fished a light, 8-weight fly rod and caught small tuna, rainbow runners, jacks, dolphin, and several other species. I had a ball.

Plan on Bad Weather

It is going to be hotter than they say, colder than they say, wetter than they say, and someone will forget the lunch. Bring the clothes you need to be comfortable in any weather.

Bring travel spin- or plug-casting gear. Some days will be so windy, you'll be better off sitting on the dock than trying to cast a fly line. I'd rather fish with spinning gear than sit around.

Use sun protection. Take an extra hat, spare polarized sunglasses, and plenty of strong sunscreen. Long-sleeved shirts designed for the tropics can reduce your exposure to the sun without making you feel uncomfortable. Consider wearing sungloves if you burn easily. Apply sunscreen several times daily. Keep sunscreen off your fingertips and palms of your hands because many sunscreen products can damage fly lines.

Pack wisely. Carry two bags and pack half of what you need in each bag. If one is lost or misdirected, the other will provide enough to fish with. Luggage tags tear off, so use duffel-type bags and label your name and address (not your phone number) on the side. Carry your reading materials, tickets, and other valuables in a backpack to keep your hands free.

Think comfort. Pack comfortable clothes for your trip, and also make sure that you have the medications and first-aid items that you need such as allergy pills, heartburn medicine, Imodium, aspirin, and lip balm. Pack things like tacky gauze tape, bandages, or a finger sock to protect the index finger of your rod hand when you are stripping line or fighting fish. Bring extra prescription glasses or contacts.

Flats Fishing

Lefty Kreh

Sight-fishing to flats species such as bonefish is exciting, but you need to be prepared for success.

Keep a clean line. Clean your line before you go out each day, and carry a line-cleaning kit with you in the boat for lines that have become sticky with salt. In a pinch you can use a cloth and fresh water to wipe the salt gum off a line.

Wear footwear that doesn't catch your fly line. I have often seen a cast fouled in midflight because the shooting line tangled in a shoe string. Many go barefoot, wear socks (to prevent burning), or wear slip-on shoes or sandals without laces.

Keep a clean boat. Whether you are with a guide or out on your own, keep the deck and general boat clean from anything that can catch your line or get in your way when you are fighting and landing a fish.

Stretch all coils from the line before making the first cast. Coils rob you of distance, are prone to tangling, and make it hard to efficiently set the hook.

Strip only the amount of line you need to cast to a fish. Too many anglers step up on the casting platform and then pull off 70 to 80 feet of line when they only need 50 to 60 feet. Any extra line on the deck is potential trouble. Master permit angler Del Brown figures 50 feet of line and a 10-foot leader is all he'll need for most situations. He makes a foot-long mark on the fly line at 50 feet. When he steps up to the casting platform, he strips off line until he reaches that mark.

Clean Your Shoes

Wash your shoe soles in the water before entering the boat. Most guides hate it when anglers track dirt into their boats. Make sure your footwear has nonskid soles.

Cast the line you have stripped from the reel and then retrieve it onto the boat deck. When you strip line from the reel, the forward end of the line falls to the bottom of the pile. Your last strip ends up on top of the pile. When you cast, the forward line comes from the bottom of the pile and tangles.

Keep line from underfoot. Casts are often ruined because you are stepping on your line. Stand a little back from the bow and drop the shooting in the well or on the main deck below the casting platform. You can also use a Line Tamer or a stripping basket, especially on windy days.

Don't stare at one spot when you search for fish. Constantly shift your eyes when you search the shallows. By staring at one place, you fail to see tiny wakes, moving fish, skipping minnows, and tailing fish. Use your peripheral vision.

Use your rod to locate the fish that the guide points out. When the guide says that the fish is at 10 o'clock (see "Telling Time," page 34) point the rod in that direction. The guide can tell you to move left or right. Before you head out to the flats, discuss with the guide how you will communicate—the clock system coupled with the rod-pointing system works well.

Don't cast until you see the fish. Unless the guide insists, never throw your fly where you think the fish is. This almost always results in a bad cast. Wait until you can spot your target.

Spare the guide. Know where the guide is when you are casting. If a fish is at 12 o'clock, don't cast until the guide has moved the rear of the boat to the side. If you cast straight ahead you will almost always hook the guide—not a good idea!

If the fish obviously doesn't see the fly, cast again. Most flats fish are sight-feeders; if you make a cast behind or too far to one side of the fish, don't continue to retrieve. Quietly pick up and cast again.

Strike by sweeping the rod sideways or with a strip-strike. Don't lift the rod tip when a fish grabs the fly. If the fish misses the fly, you've missed the strike and you may pull the fly out of the water. With a side or strip-strike, the fly remains in the water and you give the fish another chance to take it.

Beaches and Jetties

Bob Popovics

Simple strategies for the surf.

Keep it simple. The less you carry, the easier it is to walk from spot to spot, the easier it is to cast, and you are less tired at the end of the day. In New Jersey, where I fish most often, and throughout the East Coast, must-haves are a stripping basket, Korkers, bootfoot waders (stockingfoots don't keep sand out), good rain parka, polarized glasses (which also protect your eyes from stray flies), and your rod and reel. I like to store flies and other items in the large pockets on the outside of my jacket, rather than carry large bags and other things to hold tackle.

Good flies for bluefish are Bob's Bangers and chartreuse/white Surf Candies; for stripers, Bucktail Deceivers (black for night fishing, red/white during the day); and for albies, chartreuse/white Jiggies and Surf Candies.

Coil your shooting heads on wide-arbor tippet spools (such as Triple-fish Saltwater Leader) and then store the spools on your wader straps.

Ride the Wave

When you get the fish into the surf, use the water to help you land the fish quickly. Pull as the fish comes up the wave, keeping his head toward, not broadside, the beach.

Watch for people. If you are fishing on beaches or jetties, there will always be other people around. Conventional gear fishermen and other beachgoers are often not aware of how much room fly fishers need behind them. Always watch your backcast.

Ditch the rod and grab the line once you get the fish in close on a jetty. Too many anglers try to bring the fish to the rocks with their rod, which generally results in breaking the rod because of the poor angle. Put the rod down and control the fish with the line to prevent broken rods.

Take your stripping basket off or put it behind you when walking on the jetty so that you can see the gaps in between the rocks and other hazards.

Use different baskets for different conditions. No one stripping basket can do it all. For fishing in the surf or from a jetty, I like deep stripping baskets with large, quarter-size holes in the bottom to drain water quickly. For wading, I have a shallower basket without any holes that floats on the surface.

Setting the hook with the rod is generally a bad move in the salt. Hand-over-hand retrieves are great for stripping baskets, but they also have the additional advantage of ensuring that you always strip-strike the fish.

Avoid tangles in your stripping basket by placing the first 2 feet of line (the first strip on your retrieve) outside of the basket before you place the rest of the running line in the basket. This prevents disturbing the line on the bottom of the basket when you pick up the rod and begin casting.

Never bring your head into the basket—if you have to, strip it in outside of the basket.

Get the twists out of your running line while you are changing flies. When changing my fly in the surf or on the jetty, I cut off the fly and cast my line into the current while I am selecting a pattern. The pull of the current on the fly line and leader helps take the twists out. Before tying on the fly, I strip the line in through my pinched fingers to help force any coils out.

To cast effectively in the wind, you can improve your casting, use weighted flies and sinking lines, or position yourself strategically. However, when the wind is in your face, the best thing to do is reel in line and shorten up your casting distances. You are not going to be able to cast as far, so don't kill yourself trying.

New Zealand

John Randolph

Stop fantasizing about the monster fish, pristine water, and breathtaking scenery. Here are some tips to ensure a dream trip to this angling Nirvana.

Ninety percent of the largest trout taken each year in New Zealand are lake fish caught in the fall when they come out of Lake Tongariro (and other lakes) into the tributaries on their spawning runs.

Mouse populations explode about every 7 years, brought on by heavy nut crops in the beech forests, according to guide Andy Trowbridge. At this time, fishing mouse imitations can be deadly for double-digit rainbows and browns that have grown heavy from gorging on the rodents.

Some of the largest stream browns are taken in the Nelson to Hamner Springs region.

Traditionally, the North Island has been called the rainbow island and the South Island the brown island, though both islands have healthy populations of each species. The North Island has more lake fishing for huge trout and more lake-run, prespawn, large-trout fishing than the South Island.

The Te Anau area on the South Island has provided some of New Zealand's newest and best stream sight-fishing. While the area gets heavy rainfall, it is worth consideration.

NEW ZEALAND SEASONS

Season	Months	Water and Weather Conditions
Spring	October–November	rivers are bank full
Late Spring	late November–January	waters warm, rainfall can blow out rivers
Summer	January–March	rivers recede
Late summer	March	hot weather and wind
Autumn	April	low, clear water

Accurate casting (on the first cast) is important. The Achilles heel most Kiwi guides deal with is their client's bad casting. Practice casting into a hat at 30 feet before making the trip.

Learn to cast into the wind. Both the North and South Islands can have brisk winds in the late-summer dry-fly season. To cast a heavily dressed fly into the wind, overline your fast-action rod by one line weight and learn to drive the cast into the wind.

New Zealand's insect biota consists of more terrestrials than aquatic insects, including mayflies. That said, river trout look up and during summer and early fall, and they take well-presented dry flies eagerly. Nothing beats a Royal Wulff on most streams during this period. Keep it simple; improve your casting.

Hire a guide—a good one is worth his weight in gold. They can spot trout where an osprey can't.

If you are elderly, or in bad health, make sure and buy a high quality trip insurance, one that includes medivac. The investment of up to $400 for the insurance is worth the price.

A wading staff should be part of your equipment for New Zealand. Most of your fishing will be wading, and the stream bottoms are bouldery and slippery.

Camo-green lines are required by the guides, and with good reason (the trout are highly line shy). Scientific Anglers makes a good camouflage line.

Techniques and Tactics

nymphing with heavily weighted flies and indicators
dry flies come into play and trout become slightly harder to catch

prime dry-fly season; best time for backpacking and fishing
season's best terrestrial fishing; best time for backpacking and fishing
the most challenging conditions; trout are confined and easier to find; spawning browns

Fishing Etiquette

Paul Weamer

Weather, water releases, hatch activity, and trout receptiveness we cannot change. We can control the way we interact with each other while we are fishing. This important, but often overlooked, code of ethics has a tremendous impact on the quality of any fly-fishing experience.

Boating

Communicate with other fishermen. If you're not sure which side of the river someone is fishing or where to float through a pool packed with boats and waders, then ask the other fishermen how they would like you to proceed around them. Most anglers will appreciate that.

Always float behind wading anglers and other boats. If they are too close to the shore to get behind them, then quietly row to the other side of the river. Try not to row or cast while floating past them.

Get out and walk your boat. Sometimes, especially during low water, it's the only way to move through a pool or riffle without disturbing everyone else's fishing.

Learn to row in the off-season—not the peak of the Green Drake hatch. Some outfitters offer rowing courses with guides as teachers. The guide can take control of the boat during sticky situations. If you want to learn by yourself, practice on a lake or during periods of low fishing pressure.

Give wading anglers plenty of room and the right of way. Never crowd an angler who has walked into a spot. You'll have plenty of opportunities to fish other places when you're drifting. The wader has a limited amount of water. If the river is exceptionally crowded or the fishing is poor, it's okay to ask a wader if you can cast to fish rising beyond their casting range, as long your casting or boat position doesn't interfere with their fishing. Many times they will say yes, but if they do not, move on and find another fish.

Row quietly to the takeout after dark. You might be cold, hungry, and ready for a beer, but that doesn't mean everyone else has stopped fishing. It's difficult to see rising fish after sunset, and the wake and noise from a boat pushing hard to the launch compounds the problem. Judge your time and distance so you can get off of the water without rushing.

Rest Stop

You should always ask the intentions of anglers sitting on the bank or anchored in boats. They may be resting a fish. Do not begin fishing in front of, or near, a wader or another boat just because they aren't casting.

Release your anchor quietly. Hold the rope and ease it into the water. The splash from an anchor dropped into the water will scare your fish and any one else's near you.

Always be respectful on the water. Don't yell or curse loudly. Don't announce how many fish you caught and then ask a guide with clients how many they caught. A guide might be having a tough day and neither the guide nor his/her clients will appreciate your bragging.

Apologize and move on if you screw up—sooner or later everyone does. Try to learn from your mistakes.

Wading

If you're not sure where an upriver boat is headed, then politely reveal where you are fishing and ask the rower to go behind you, if possible. Let your intentions be known—no one can read your mind.

Pick one side of the river to fish and do not switch sides when a boat approaches. Too many times wading anglers cast to one side of the river and quickly cast the other direction, after it's too late for an upriver boat to correct its course. Boats are maneuverable, but changing direction quickly in moving water can be difficult and sometimes impossible.

Stop casting when a boat is behind you. Sometimes it's necessary for a boat to float very close to you to avoid spooking your fish. I've seen careless waders unintentionally hook boaters on their backcast by not paying attention.

continued on page 196

Fishing Etiquette continued

Wade quietly. You'll catch more fish and will not disturb those fishing around you.

Cross the river well above or below another angler whenever possible.

Never stand directly across the river from another angler unless you are fishing a large, deep pool. He may be easing his way out to your fish or may be able to cast farther than you can. Stand across from an angler fishing a big pool only if he cannot reach the fish you are casting to. If you're not sure he can reach the fish, ask.

Never trespass across private property no matter how good the fishing is on the other side.

Breathing Room

Solitude is priceless, and it's a great gift to give yourself or another fisherman whenever possible. If you're lucky enough to be fishing the river on a day with few other anglers, give at least half a pool to another fisherman.

Whether wading or floating, don't "relieve" yourself within plain sight of houses or buildings. You wouldn't like someone doing that in your yard.

Parking Area and Boat Launches

Don't park in boat turn-around areas, even though they are often closer to the river than the parking areas. Several times, I have seen anglers unable to launch their boat due to a parked car in the turn-around. Occasionally, I have watched drift-boat owners almost hit a parked car in these areas while trying to launch their boats.

Do not block the boat-launch areas. Often anglers drive their cars onto the ramp at a boat launch, just to get a look at the river. I have done this myself, occasionally, but only at appropriate times. It's not appropriate to park on a boat launch ramp during the river's busy season. Don't drive onto a boat launch at this time of year unless you're planning to launch a boat.

Boating anglers may retrieve their vehicles, and load their boats, in the order they arrived at the boat launch. It's common, at the most popular launches during the peak season, for a line of anglers to be anchored at a launch, waiting for their turn to remove their boats from the river. Everyone's in a hurry and wants to get home, to eat, to get dry, to do a lot of things. But you must remain patient. I have witnessed near fistfights between anglers who ran to get their car, out of turn, and those still waiting at the launch.

When it is your turn to remove your boat at the launch, get your car, get your boat, and get out. Don't have a talk with your friends, break down your rods, pack your gear, or have a cigarette. You can do all these things after you're off the launch. Guides have to get home, shower, eat, make lunches, and check their gear and boats for the next day's trip—all before they can go to sleep. Other anglers may not be guides, but they may have to work the next day, or maybe they need to get home to be with their families. You may be on vacation—just don't spend it on top of the boat ramp.

Don't shine your headlights toward the river from the boat launch. You will ruin the night vision of any anglers still fishing and blind those trying to navigate to the launch.

Finding Great Lakes Solitude

Rick Kustich

When fish are in, the challenge is not in catching them, it's finding some elbow room. Here's how to beat the crowds.

Prime time is late October and November, and again in March and April. Fish during the "off months." Steelhead, browns, and salmon run as early as August on some streams, and you can have good fishing in midwinter as long as the rivers are free of ice.

Look for cool weather and rain storms that raise stream levels and bring fish in early (September and early October) and late (April and May) in the season. In winter (December–February), days when the air temperatures are above freezing are best.

Fish in foul weather during prime time. If it's cold or raining, there will be less people on the stream. Avoid sunny days.

If water rises fast and there's a lot of debris in it, such as leaves, then the fishing shuts down. But once water stabilizes and starts to drop, you can often hook fish in murky water by targeting their holding lies.

Fish late in the day. Most Great Lakes anglers get on the water at the crack of dawn, and the catch-and-keep anglers leave the stream after they fill their limits. Steelhead become active again in the low light of evening.

Dropping and Clearing

Fish when water clarity is dropping and clearing during prime time. That might mean hopping over to a stream that was turbid the day before on the off chance that you can be one of the first there when it starts to clear and the fish go on the grab.

The farther you walk, the better able you are to get away from crowds. You can also float larger streams for solitude.

Fish overlooked water. Most anglers concentrate on the pools, but you can catch fish in small slots and pocketwater and by swinging flies through tailouts.

Fish rivers that typically receive lower annual runs than surrounding rivers. Anglers tend to gravitate to the greatest opportunity to catch fish. Rivers that are not stocked at all and depend on strays from other rivers or on natural reproduction will generally experience lower runs. This is also true of rivers that receive lower plantings than surrounding rivers.

Fish big water. Many anglers are intimidated by bigger sections of river. With two-handed rods and Spey techniques, all water in the Great Lakes region can effectively be covered.

SPECIES OTHER THAN TROUT

Steelhead

Lani Waller

Be there when they are. Get reliable information anywhere you can. If you drive along a river, you can always tell if the fish are there by the number of vehicles parked by the side of the road.

Most steelhead prefer flies that are moving fairly slowly—about half the current speed. You can fish a steelhead fly too fast, but it is hard to fish it too slowly.

Half the summer-run steelhead that rise to your dry fly should actually take it. If significantly fewer than that take your fly, it means your dry fly is too large.

Pink is a great color for a steelhead fly. In dirty water, hot pink reflects any light penetrating the surface.

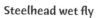

Steelhead wet fly

Steelhead prefer to lie close to shore if the current is right, if the water is at least 3 feet deep, and if they have not been disturbed by wading anglers. Fish that water first before wading out to your armpits.

Use fly lines with interchangeable tips to modify the depth you are fishing. Not all runs are created equal.

In the end, a deep fly produces the most strikes.

In clear water, take larger, or more, steps between casts. Slow down when water visibility gets around 2 feet.

Search for fish you cannot see with larger flies that push more water, making it easier for the maximum numbers of fish to see the fly, under the widest range of water depths, surface textures, clarity, and from the greatest distances.

Close the deal on a fish that has risen to a searching pattern but refused it with a smaller fly that pushes less water and makes a smaller surface disturbance. Judge the fly by the size of the surface disturbance it makes on the water, and not the size of the fly. The actual volume of the fly's body is usually only relevant in places where it can be clearly seen by a temperamental or "fussy" fish.

Fast Walk

Most steelhead prefer water speeds about the same as a fast walk. Avoid fast rapids and riffles and slow or stagnant water.

The greater the difference between the fly a fish just refused and the next one you show it, the more likely it will take it. So, if the fish rises to a greased #6 Muddler, and you want to short-circuit the process, don't choose a #8 Muddler as your next fly. Immediately go to a wet fly.

There are no accidents in nature, and no mistakes—only patterns of cause and effect. Everything happens for a reason, and the more of those reasons and connections you know, the clearer your understanding of the patterns of nature become. So remember everything you see when you hook a steelhead—the depth, color, and speed of the water; the light and water temperature.

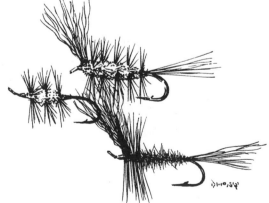

Steelhead dry flies

How to Catch Trophy Smallmouth Bass

Bob Clouser

To catch large bass consistently requires special techniques.

Improve your casting. You need to be able to make long, accurate casts—often with heavy flies. Learn to make only one (or two, at most) backcasts to present the fly. Lines with heavy front tapers help you cast large flies great distances with minimal false casts.

Fish in big-bass water and focus on big-bass habitat. Big bass prefer areas with deep water, moving currents, and structure with large rocks, sunken trees, large logs, or some other debris that provides a place to escape to—and a hiding place from which to ambush food.

Find unpressured water—whether that means being the first on the water or floating or walking to water that doesn't get hit hard.

Fish early or fish late. At these hours, there are fewer anglers on the water to spook the fish, and large bass are often feeding—sometimes in shallow water.

Hunt heads and cast only to the largest fish. Don't spend time on the splashy risers, look for swells or swirls, or better yet, rolling fish. Small dimples can sometimes mean large fish, and it pays to watch a rising fish to try and determine size. If fishing in clear water where you can spot the fish, don't waste time casting to smaller bass—even though this may be fun, you may not be prepared for a big one when you see it.

Be patient. To catch big bass, wait for them. Smaller bass generally

Give Them the Groceries

Big bass eat big flies. Small flies are fine for small fish, but lure the lunkers with large patterns.

begin rising first, and if you start casting to them, the bigger bass may spook and never rise. Stake out an area and wait—like a hunter waits for his prey.

Be stealthy. Avoid bright clothing and reflective tackle. Pull or drop anchor quietly. Wade slowly so that you don't create a lot of disturbance on the water.

Have good timing. Spring, when bass are spawning, and fall, when bass feed heavily to prepare for winter, are the best times to consistently catch trophies. I prefer not to fish for spawning bass and focus my efforts on fall fishing.

Pay attention to water temperature. Even though spring and fall are prime times, when the water temperatures rise above 85 degrees, big bass need to feed constantly because their metabolisms are at the highest point. On many rivers, you will see them chasing baitfish during a hot summer day.

Fish the rise. Not hatches, rising water. When the water rises as a result of rain or other factors, big bass go on the prowl for the abundance of food that becomes available as water disturbs the bottom debris and knocks insects and crayfish loose from their crevices. High water pushes baitfish out of the heavy current in the center of a river toward the margins along the shore. When baitfish concentrate in these areas, bass move in to feed on them.

Look for mudding carp. Carp feed and disturb the stream bottom and bass often follow behind them, eating crayfish and insects that are kicked up. This is one of the best ways I know to consistently catch large bass in the heat of summer.

Stay sharp. Be prepared to catch the big ones. Take care of your body like you take care of your gear. Stay sharp mentally by drinking enough water and eating nutritious snacks; dress for a wide range of weather conditions. Maintain and care for your gear throughout the year, and check to make sure your hook points are sharp and your tippets aren't frayed or nicked throughout the day. Fish with tackle appropriate for large fish. Always ask yourself, what am I going to do if I hook a monster? Is my tackle up for the job?

Stillwater Carp

Brad Befus

Besides lakes and reservoirs, many golf course, park, and farm ponds contain carp (most likely grass carp) because they help control weed growth.

Target carp feeding in the shallows. Though carp will feed in deeper water, shallow-water fishing is not only exciting but easier to present your fly to a fish that is actively feeding.

In the spring, dark-bottomed bays heat faster, attracting carp.

Klooping fish feed on the surface with an audible popping or sucking noise. They may be eating anything from cottonwood seeds, berries, terrestrials, or aquatic insects. Lead surface feeders so they intercept your fly.

Carp chasing
crayfish

Tailing fish are active feeders, rooting along the bottom like redfish, and are only interested in what is right in front of them. You must place your fly within 6 to 8 inches of the fish's window of sight.

Hellraisers are most often spawning fish, identified by their splashes and wallows. These fish are hard to catch and you should focus your efforts on active feeders.

Cruisers—carp swimming along at mid-depth—fall into two categories: spooked and roaming fish. Spooked fish are swimming fast and erratically and aren't worth your efforts. Roaming fish (singles or packs) are worth watching because one or more of them may start to feed.

A slight twitch of any pattern sometimes provokes a strike.

Pick individual targets rather than casting into the middle of large packs of carp. It sometimes pays to watch the fish before casting in case they start to feed.

Walk slowly and try not to push too much water when wading. If in a boat, use a push pole, not a motor.

Strip-strike to give the carp another chance to take the fly if it misses it the first time.

Cast to Feeding Fish

Spend your time casting to feeding carp, not cruising, sunbathing, or spooked fish. Feeding carp are most often either klooping (feeding on the surface) or rooting on the bottom, with their tails tipped and heads down.

West Coast Stripers

Dan Blanton

Advice from an expert guide on the West Coast's finest fishery and good general tips for all saltwater fishing. Visit danblanton.com for more information on this and a wide range of topics.

Hire a guide for one or two outings to help shorten the learning curve if you have never fished San Francisco Bay or the Delta. Some hire two or three different guides to learn more than one approach to the fisheries.

You can cover more water from a boat since shore fishing is limited on the Bay and Delta.

Get good charts learn a section of water at a time. Very important, too, is a good fish finder/depth sounder to locate structure, holes, drop-offs, weed lines, and, of course, bait and fish.

The best tides for fishing the Bay system are the "Neap" tides, which occur on a quarter moon phase. The reason is that the flats where you'll have the greatest chances of success will remain flooded during prime morning time since there will be less exchange of water from high to low tide. Avoid big tidal swings that occur on "Spring" tides.

Delta tides are not as critical, but you do want moving water with the major tide occurring during the daylight hours. On full-moon periods you can still catch fish during the day, but the major tidal flow will be at night and the bass feed most heavily at that time. Fishing at night on the Bay is illegal, but night fishing is permitted on the Delta.

Use 8- to 9-weight rods since you'll be casting fairly large

Blanton's Whistler

and heavy flies. Reels should have a good drag and hold at least 150 yards of backing.

Fast-sinking shooting heads or integrated heads are the most useful lines. You'll also want a slow-sinker for shallower waters, such as a type II or III shooting head. A floating shooting head with an intermediate shooting line is a great choice for tossing poppers, Crease Flies, and Gurglers—upline by at least two weights when using shooting heads. Put 50-pound braided loops on all the lines for attaching leaders and backing. A stripping basket or tub (vertical line management device) helps. I like to use 8 feet of 20-pound Berkley Big Game looped to the braided loop using a surgeon's loop or a Bimini twist loop for a leader with sinking lines. I attach the fly with a Kreh nonslip loop knot.

Top flies: Blanton's Jig Hook Flashtail Whistler; Blanton's Jig Hook Flashtail Clouser; Sar-Mul-Mac; Half & Half; Lefty's Deceiver; Ron Dong Crease Fly; Blados Crease Fly; and Gurglers. Top sizes and colors: 2/0 and 3/0 in white/chartreuse; white/pink/purple; white/brown; white/gray; and black. Bulky flies that push water and sink fast are more productive in turbid waters.

The best retrieves are a mix of full- and half-arm extensions, with several pauses during the retrieve (also called the stop-and-drop technique) to allow the fly to sink like an injured baitfish. Make the fly jump to push some water and attract attention. Short, twitchy, Woolly Bugger retrieves don't work well. Stopping and dropping is particularly important in the Delta once the water temperature falls under 50 degrees.

The right retrieve is often more important than the fly. Always retrieve the fly until the leader hits the rod tip. Hover it on the surface a moment before lifting it for a recast. It's amazing how many fish hit at the last second just as you're lifting the fly.

The best months to fish the Bay are March and April and again in September through November. Midsummer isn't as productive since most of the fish are in the ocean. The best fishing in the Delta begins in September, with October, November, and December producing best; and again in March. If I only had two months to fish the Delta, it would be October and November.

Shad

Brian Wiprud

Shad have quietly been providing anglers from California to Connecticut with amazing fly-rod sport.

Location is everything. Typically tails of rapids are the most likely places to find large numbers of shad. They gather in the pools overnight and ascend the rapids in daylight.

Rising water temperatures between 55 and 72 degrees are ideal; conversely, cooling water works in your favor any time the river reaches 73 degrees, the temperature at which shad spawn and are less inclined to feed. A cool rain or colder tributary that lowers the river tributary can turn distracted spawning fish back to schooling fish ready to strike.

Shad continue to move upriver in bright sun and in the middle of the day. I've often read or heard that shad prefer to move in low light, but my best days are sunny, cloudless days between 10 A.M. and 2 P.M. Early mornings are often productive, but shad drop into deeper water in the pool as the sun rises. When they become accustomed to the brighter conditions (around 10 A.M.), they once again start to move up river into the shallow water of the rapids.

When fishing water 5 feet deep or less, a floating line and a standard downstream swing is the best presentation.

Weight is the most important attribute of a shad fly. It must be heavy enough to reach the fish. If shad are moving toward your fly, but not hitting, add more weight.

Fly color is often debated, but you can't go wrong with pink, red, orange, or chartreuse.

Precise imitations are less effective than simple patterns that accentuate the basic visual qualities of small crustaceans, primarily their translucent, almost-clear bodies and a small dab of color (either green or pink) in their upper carapace.

Tie or buy flies that ride hook point up to increase the number of hookups in the roof of the mouth (shad's lips are thin and tear easily) and keep the hook point from dulling on the river bottom.

Look for Seams

Shad schools in the ocean often corral prey along current seams and at thermal boundaries. Locations such as strong current seams and tributary confluences that mimic these conditions in rivers can collect large numbers of fish and cause them to feed opportunis-

Index

accuracy
  exercises for, 6
  with shooting lines, 3
  with sinking lines, 3
Albolene, 74
amadou, 75
American Fishing Tackle Manufacturers
  Association line standards chart, 107
Ames, Dave, "A Guide's Thoughts on
  Stealth and Presentations," 57
anchors, 55
Anderson, George, "Fishing Pods,"
  158–159
ants, 165
Aquastealth. *See* rubber soles
Atlantic salmon
  handling, 66
  striking, 59

backcasts
  Ed Jaworowski's tips for, 14–15
  wind at your back, 15
backcountry fishing, Ross Purnell's tips
  for, 182–183
backing, 118–119
barbless hooks, 59, 63
barracuda, handling and releasing, 67
bass
  Bob Clouser's tips for, 202–203
  handling and releasing, 66
  weighing, 71

bamboo rods, Jerry Kustich's tips for,
  124–125
Barr, John, "Trico Time," 152–153
beaches, Bob Popovics' tips for,
  190–191
bears, 179–180
Beck, Barry and Cathy, "Better Fishing
  Photography," 68–69
Befus, Brad, "Stillwater Carp," 204–205
bendbacks, 80
bicycle rig, 77
Bisharat, George, "Kiwi Lessons,"
  42–43
Blanton, Dan, "West Coast Stripers,"
  206–207
bluefish
  good flies for, 190
  handling and releasing, 67
boats
  casting from, 51
  cleaning and disinfecting, 131
  etiquette, 194–195, 196
  flats fishing, 188–189
  lightning, 167
  presentations, 57
  preventing tangles in, 12
  stillwater setup, 55
  streamer fishing, 82–83
bonefish, handling and releasing, 67
boots. *See* wading boots
braided loops, 114–115

Cambridge, Joe, "Frosty Freestoners,"
  172–173
carp
  Brad Befus' tips for, 204–205
  mudding, 203
casting
  accuracy, 3
  backcasts, 14–15
  cracking the whip, 2
  distance, 8–9
  double haul, 8
  Lefty Kreh's principles, 4
  practice, 2
  on the shelf, 7
  Spey-casting, 16–17
  taming tangles, 12
  tailing loops, 3
  tandem flies, 18
  tightening loops, 4–5
  weight, 10–11
  wind, 13–15
catfish, handling and releasing, 66
Caucci's Krazy Glue Splice, 116
cauterizing tool, 88
Chan, Brian, "Stillwater Trout," 52–56
cleaning fly lines, 9, 38, 103–104
clear-tip lines, 51
cleats, 133
Clouser, Bob
  "Casting Weight," 10–11
  "Clouser's Quick-Turnover Bass
    Leader," 96
  "How to Catch Trophy Smallmouth
    Bass," 202–203
cracking the whip, 2
clinch knot, 102
  forceps with, 100
  quick clinch, 99
cobia, handling and releasing, 67
comfort grip, 64
Craven, Charlie, "Improved Slip Knot,"
  136–137
crickets, 164

Didymo, 130
dirty water, techniques for, 34–35
distance casting, 8–9
  underlining for, 20
double haul. See haul
drag, 38–40
dry-and-dropper. See tandem flies
dry flies, 74–75
Duncan loop, 77

eddies, 41
egg patterns, 164
etiquette
  in boats, 194–195
  parking area and boat launches,
    196–197
  wading, 195–196

false albacore
  good flies for, 190
  handling and releasing, 67
felt sole, 133
ferrules, stuck, 120
fighting fish, 60–62
finding fish
  Scott Sanchez's tips for big water,
    30–31
Fletch Dry, use with dry flies, 74
floatants
  for dry flies, 74–75
  for small flies, 76
fly boxes, 87–88
fly lines
  AFTMA line standards, 107
  cleaning, 103–104
  marking, 106
  organizing, 106
  removing twist, 104
  repairing, 105
  for stillwaters, 55
  weighing, 107
foam, 28
footwear
  surf fishing, 26
  wading boot soles, 133
  wet wading, 27

footwork, casting and, 9
forceps
  with built-in scissors, 141
  tying knots with, 100
forward cast, stopping the rod, 3
Frog's Fanny
  and dry flies 74–76
  and nymphs, 79

Galland, Dick, "Wading Basics," 22–24
Garth's GSP splice, 117
Gawesworth, Simon, "Spey-Casting,"
  16–17
grass leader, 7
grasshoppers, 164
Great Lakes, Rick Kustich's tips for,
  198–199
grip, improving, 6
grip, rod
  cleaning, 126
  repair, 126
GSP
  cat's paw with, 119
  Garth's GSP Splice, 117, 118–119
  simplified GSP splice, 119
guides, 180–181
gulpers, 156–157

handling fish
  for photography, 69
  by species, 66–67
Harvey, George
  slack-line leader, 95
hatches
  Charles Meck's tips for, 150–151
  matching, 148
  reading riseforms, 154–157
  timing, 149
  Tricos, 152–153
hauling, 5, 8–9
  triple haul, 13
headlamp, 47
high water, techniques for, 35–36

hooks
  debarbing, 84
  removing, 90–91
  sharpening, 84–86
Hula hoop, practicing with, 6

insect repellant, 166
indicators
  balloons, 140
  recycled fly line, 139
  yarn, 134–139

Jaworowski, Ed, "Better Backcasts,"
  14–15
jetties, Bob Popovics' tips for, 190–191

Keelin, Tom, 70
knots, 98–102
  Chapstick with, 101
  clinch knot basics, 102
  forceps with, 100
  improved blood knot, 101
  quick clinch, 99
  testing, 98
Krazy Glue splice, 116
Kreh, Lefty
  casting principles, 4
  "Flats Fishing," 188–189
  "Improve Your Double Haul," 8
  "Saltwater Travel Tips," 186–187
Kumiski, Captain John, "Spotting
  Saltwater Fish," 36–37
Kustich, Jerry, "Bamboo Rods,"
  124–125
Kustich, Rick, "Finding Great Lakes
  Solitude," 198–199

Lawson, Mike, "Tips for Catching
  Selective, Rising Trout," 160–161
leaders, 92–97
  Clouser's Quick-Turnover Bass Leader,
  96
  grass leader, 7
  Harvey's Slack-Line Leader, 95
  store-bought leaders, unwrapping, 93
  straightening, 93

leaks, repairing waders, 131–132
lightning, 167
Line Tamer, 12
Loon Outdoors UV Cure, 131
loop-to-loop connections, 48, 97–98
loops
    braided loops, 114–115
    whipped loop, 108–109
    Whitlock's Zap-A-Gap Loop, 110–111

Mayer, Landon, "Sight-Fishing Secrets,"
    32–33
McLennan, Jim
    "Drift-Boat Streamer Tactics," 82–83
    "Nymphing without Indicators," 78
Meck, Charles
    "Mastering the Hatches," 150–151
    "Tandem Flies," 18
    looped-leader flies, 76
    phenological fly, 162–163
mending, 39
mosquitoes, 166
mousetrap, practicing with, 6
movable dropper, 77
musky
    handling, 66
    weighing, 70

nets, 65, 70
New Zealand mudsnails, 130–131
New Zealand, 42–43
    John Randolph's tips for, 192–193
night fishing, 47–49
nymphing
    striking, 59
    without indicators, 78
nymphs, 79

overhang, 11
overlining rods, 19, 107

permit, handling and releasing, 67
phenological fly, 162–163
photographing fish, Barry and Cathy
    Beck's tips for, 68–69

pike
    handling, 66
    weighing, 70
pods, George Anderson's tips for,
    158–159
polarized glasses
    choosing right lens, 144
    sight fishing and, 32
Popovics, Bob, "Beaches and Jetties,"
    190–191
Powergum, 76
principles of casting, 4
puffball nymphing rig, indicator for, 135
Purnell, Ross, "Backcountry Fishing,"
    182–183

Randolph, John, "New Zealand,"
    192–193
reach cast, 39–40
redfish
    handling and releasing, 67
    spotting, 37
reels
    drags, 128
    maintenance, 127
releasing fish, 63–67
    by species, 66–67
    reviving fish, 64
riseforms, reading, 154–157
rods
    assembling, 121–122
    bamboo, 124–125
    care of, 122
    cleaning grips, 126
    freeing stuck ferrules, 120
    purchasing, 126
    traveling with, 123
    rope casting, 5
    rubber soles, 133
    runoff, 164. See also high water

saltwater
    Bob Popovics on beaches and jetties,
        190–191
    Dan Blanton on West Coast stripers,
        206–207

Lefty Kreh on flats fishing, 188–189
maintenance of reels, 127–128
releasing saltwater species, 67
spotting fish, 36–37
travel tips, 186–187
two-hand retrieve, 44
wading, 25–26
Sanchez, Scott, "Finding Fish in Big
    Water," 30–31
Scotchguard, use with dry flies, 74
selective trout, Mike Lawson's tips for,
    160–161
shad, Brian Wiprud's tips for, 208–209
shark, handling and releasing, 67
shooting heads, 107
    joining, 116
    storing, 190, 191
shooting line
    accuracy, 3
    on backcast, 8
    preventing tangles, 9
sight fishing
    Landon Mayer's tips for, 32–33
    saltwater fish, 36–37
    telling time, 34
sinking lines
    accuracy with, 3
    casting, 10–11
    defeating wind, 13
    roll casting, 10
small flies, 75–76
small streams
    casting, 19
    strategies for, 45–46
smallmouth, Bob Clouser's tips for,
    202–203. See also bass
smell, trout's sense of, 57
snags, 89–90
snook
    handling and releasing, 67
    night fishing for, 48
solitude, 29
Spey casting
    grass leader for, 7
    Simon Gawesworth's tips for, 16–17

splices
    Caucci's Krazy Glue Splice, 116
    Garth's GSP Splice, 117
    Whitlock's Zap-A-Gap Splice,
        112–113
split shot, 140–141
spring, 162–164
stack cast, 39
stealth
    Dave Ames' tips for, 57
    New Zealand lessons, 42–43, 49–51
steaming flies, 89
steelhead
    handling, 66
    Lani Waller's tips for, 200–201
    Rick Kustich's tips for Great Lakes,
        198–199
    striking, 59
    weighing, 71
stillwaters
    Brian Chan's tips for, 52–56
    carp in, 204–205
streamers
    Jim Mclennan's tips for, 82–83
    two-hand retrieve, 44, 79–81
stretching line, 8, 12, 105–106
    removing line twist, 191
strike indicators. See indicators
striking fish, 58–59
stripers
    Dan Blanton's tips for, 206–207
    good flies for, 190, 207
    handling and releasing, 67
stripping baskets
    and distance, 8
    Line Tamer, 12
    making your own, 143
    in the surf, 26
    tips, 143
strip-strike, 58
stroke, improving, 6–7
summer, 165–167
sun protection, 166
sunfish, weighing, 71
sunglasses. See polarized glasses
surf, wading in the, 25–26

tailing fish, 63
tailing loops
  curing, 3
  on backcast, 15
tailout, 25
tailwaters, wading, 26–27
tandem flies
  beating drag with, 40
  bicycle rig, 77
  Charles Meck's tips for, 18
  looped leader, 76
  movable dropper, 77
  seeing your fly, 41, 43, 76–77
  streamers, 80
tangles, preventing, 9, 10, 12–13
tarpon
  bowing to, 61
  handling and releasing, 67
terrestrials, 164. *See also* ants; crickets;
  grasshoppers
tightening loops, 4–5
time system, for pointing out fish, 34
tippets, 92–94
  loops with, 97
travel
  general tips, 176–177
  Lefty Kreh's tips for saltwater,
    186–187
  researching destinations, 177–179
Tricos
  John Barr's tips for, 152–153, 165
trip insurance, 177
triple haul, 13
trout
  handling, 66
  weighing, 71
twists, removing, 191

underlining rods, 20
uplining rods, 19, 107
USDA hardiness zone maps, 149
UV Cure, 131

viewing lanes, 32

waders
  care and cleaning, 129
  disinfecting, 130–131
  repairing, 131–132
wading boots
  care and comfort, 132–133
  choosing the best sole, 133
  in winter, 171
wading
  Dick Galland's tips for, 22–24
  wading the surf, 25–26
  wading tailwaters, 26
  wet wading, 27
wading staff, 21
walking the dog, 38
Waller, Lani, "Steelhead," 200–201
water haul
  double, 11
  single, 10
water windows, 32
Weamer, Paul, "Fishing Etiquette,"
  194–197
weighing fish, 70–71
  bass, 71
  pike and musky, 70
  sunfish and crappie, 71
  trout, salmon, and steelhead, 71
weighted flies
  casting practice, 2
  accuracy, 3
  Bob Clouser's tips for, 10–11
whipped loop, 108–109
Whitlock's Zap-A-Gap Loop, 110–111
Whitlock's Zap-A-Gap Splice, 112–113
wind
  at your back, 15
  on your casting arm, 14
  in your face, 13
  sinking line, 13
  underlining, 20
winter, 169–173
  staying warm in, 170–171
  wading, 21
Wiprud, Brian, "Shad," 208–209